WHITE SIDEWALKS

WHITE SIDEWALKS

TALES OF MAVIS STREET — 1963

ANTI-POETRY
BY STARK HUNTER

Copyright 2021 by Stark Hunter

Paperback ISBN: 978-1-63337-511-6
E-Book ISBN: 978-1-63337-407-2
LCCN: 2021910563

Published by Mind Tavern Books

All rights reserved. No part of this book may be reproduced or transmitted in any form or by any means, electronic or mechanical, including photocopying, recording, or by any information storage and retrieval system, without permission in writing from the copyright owners.

Photographs from the Stark Hunter Collection.

INTRODUCTION

THIS BOOK WAS COMPOSED IN 4 WEEKS — November-December, 2020. Though there are 53 titled anti-poems in this work, I consider White Sidewalks to be one continuous poem.

In these word paintings that I have set, there are impressionistic-like memories of childhood, presented as a series of memory-dances in a literary ballet of sorts; all set to the popular music of the time — 1963.

The mind excursions that form this nostalgic quilt came into existence during the daunting times of Covid-19. Most of what is written here was composed at all hours of the waking day inside my cold garage; but mostly in the late hours. The poet's "psychological time machine" flies often and much better after midnight.

To all my millions of non-readers: Please consider this work as just an "escape-poem" for the poet, and for you, from a world closed down.

As for whether all this is true is entirely a moot point. In today's world, nothing is true, although I claim about seventy-five percent of this is true. The other twenty-five percent is "madness tempered" — by creative writing.

Quant à savoir si tout cela est vrai, il est entièrement discutable. Dans le monde d'aujourd'hui, rien n'est vrai, même si j'affirme que soixante-quinze pour cent de cela est vrai. Les vingt-cinq pour cent restants sont «tempérés par la folie» - par l'écriture créative.

En cuanto a si todo esto es cierto es completamente discutible. En el mundo de hoy, nada es cierto, aunque afirmo que alrededor del setenta y cinco por ciento de esto es cierto. El otro veinticinco por ciento está "templado por la locura" por la escritura creativa.

STARK HUNTER, 2021

TO THORNTON WILDER

TABLE OF CONTENTS

PART ONE: "UNDER THE SILVER CONSTELLATIONS"

1: "I Think It's Because I'm Catholic" 1
2: "I Wonder If I'll Get A Free Stick Today?" 4
3: "No Need To Look Inside There" 6
4: "I Like Blonde Kids" 8
5: "I Like Living On Mavis Street" 10
6: "As Missus Sabatini Smiles" 13
7: "I Like To Play Army" 15
8: "Maybe Mister Gumm Has Extras" 17
9: "I Really Don't Get It" 21
10: "I Don't Think That's True At All" 24

INTERMISSION 1

11: "I Like Twinkies" 28
12: "Kenny Stultz Is Laughing Now" 30
13: "Dennis Nelson Hates Stew" 32
14: "God Has Left The Building" 35
15: "The Missus Finds A Surprise" 38
16: "Larry Stultz Cannot Believe His Eyes" 41
17: "As Young As Shirley Sisson And Rover" 44
18: "I Like Liverwurst" 46
19: "I Like Miss Jane" 49
20: "The Smoking Mothers Are Clapping" 52

INTERMISSION 2

21: "I Can See All This Without My Curtain" 56
22: "Now The Missus Lights Up A Salem" 59
23: "The Mister Puts Down His Crossword Puzzle" 62
24: "It Flies Away Without Its Head" 66
25: "Fleeing Quickly From The Impala" 68
26: "I Like Library Day" 72

27: "Shirley Sisson Has A Bigger Chest" 76
28: "He Says Kenny Stultz Is A Luck-Out" 78
29: "It Seems They're Scratching The Sky" 80
30: "I'm Happy Kenny Stultz Is Still Alive" 82

INTERMISSION 3
31: "Why Are All You Kids Locked Out?" 86
32: "I Want Eddie Magehee's Baseball Cards" 88
33: "Life Is Good In 1963" 91
34: "I Once Wet My Pants in 1956" 95
35: "Now I'm Standing On Randy Robertson's Fence" 99
36: "This Is The Cruelest Thing I Have Ever Seen" 102

PART TWO: "TWILIGHT CONVOCATIONS" PAS DE DEUX
37: "I Am Not Eleven Years Old Anymore" 107
38: "I Am Seeing Ghosts On The White Sidewalks" 109
39: "I Can Still Hear Them Screaming At Each Other" 113
40: "Dennis Nelson Is Dressed In His Funeral Suit" 115

INTERMISSION 4
41: "Life Was Good In 1957" 120
42: "These Twilight Convocations Haven't Ended" 123
43: "I Learned Many Things From My Mother" 125
44: "I Asked If I Was Still Dreaming" 128
45: "Back To When Life Turned Differently" 129
46: "Hey Mister Gumm. Any Extras?" 131
47: "I See A Pall Mall Cigarette Dangling From His Lips" 133
48: "Life Is Wicked, Man. Remember That" 136
49: "I Finally Tell Jeff Sabatini I'm Sorry" 139
50: "In The Middle Of The Old Model Market Parking Lot" 141
51: "They Will Tell You Volumes In Silence" 143
52: "The Vapor Is Gone" 145
53: "I Like My Dad" 147
About the Author 151

PART ONE
"UNDER THE SILVER CONSTELLATIONS"

THE GUYS — 1963
PICTURED: STARK HUNTER, LARRY STULTZ AND KENNY STULTZ

1
"I THINK IT'S BECAUSE I'M CATHOLIC"

I am walking.
I am 11 times around the yellow pancake.
It's 1963 and I live with my Catholic family.
My dad is 46 years old.
My mom is 42, and as my brother nears his sixteenth go-round,
well,
I am walking…

Watch me as I flat-foot it up this white sidewalk…
Mavis Street is crowded with loud children.
Loud white children, running in bee-lines from house to tree,
From front-yard to back-yard.
These trees are good friends.
They can keep secrets.
They know when to be quiet,
Know when to shield the sun on hot summer days.

I know most of the people living on this street…
I can tell you their names.
Over there in that house. See it?
Eddie Magehee lives inside there.
He's a big kid with red hair and a deep voice.
I like his Schwinn Racer.
Next door is Miss Jane's house.
She lives with her husband who looks a lot younger than Miss Jane.
She sits on her front porch a lot and smokes cigarettes.

WHITE SIDEWALKS

Next to her live the three Wooster brothers; Stevie, Robbie and Gary.
Those boys are always up to something, and their mom is strict.
Does no good I guess.
Their dad is a businessman.
He wears nice suits.

I can hear my footsteps on the sidewalk.
Hear 'em?
They sound like someone beating two small drums.

There's Missus Hope on her front porch.
She has varicose veins on her legs.
She is always wearing an apron,
And her kitchen smells like baked cookies.

Now I can see Missus Sabatini through her little kitchen window;
She's doing the dishes with a smile on her face.
I wonder why she smiles so much.
Mister Sabatini drives the black truck.
He has dark skin and short black hair.
My mother says many Italians have olive-colored skin.
I like Mister Sabatini.
He is always smiling like Missus Sabatini.

On the other side of the street—
I see Erik Nelson folding newspapers.
He has blond hair and listens to his transistor radio as he counts.
He secretly listens to the forbidden KRLA and the Tune-Dex.
Missus Nelson has forbidden rock and roll music to all her children.
Missus Hilliard, next door, is in her kitchen too.

She is not smiling, not lost in thought, like Missus Sabatini.
Her dark-haired daughter, Kandace, is a dancing beauty.
I can see her down their driveway in their green backyard.
She is in a white leotard, pirouetting like a dream fairy.

Next is the green house of the Sissons;
Living here are the Mister and the Missus,
And their three children: Shirley, Judy and Herbert.
The Mister is a quiet man.
But he wears his hair uniquely.
It is long and ratted up, and I am sure
A family of sparrows could nest in it.
The Missus reminds me of a casino waitress in Reno.
But she is a pretty lady.
Shirley and Judy are big girls with boyfriends.
Shirley likes to spend time inside her boyfriend's Studebaker kissing him.
Herbert is a sissy. He never comes out to play.

Down the street across from the Magehee' house lives Missus White.
She likes to suntan in the nude.
Nobody's seen her yet, but everybody knows about it.

I like all these people.
And they like me because, well,
I think it's because I'm Catholic.

2
"I WONDER IF I'LL GET A FREE STICK TODAY?"

I am still walking…
Look.
I can see the Nelsons driving down Mavis Street—
Inside their Rambler station wagon.
Mister Nelson is driving—
The red-haired Missus Nelson is at his side.
In the back are their Catholic daughters:
Sharon, Kathleen, freckled Valerie and Christina.
Their two boys are absent.
Where's Dennis?
He is my good friend with freckles too.
They came to Mavis from Massachusetts.
I like the Red Sox as much as they do.

This sidewalk is smooth and worn.
I like to ride my Schwinn on the sidewalk.
Me and Kenny Stultz, and his little brother, Larry—
We ride bikes and flexies on these sidewalks a lot.

Now we're nearing the Bliss House,
Home of two little girls, Susan and Marilyn.
I see them a lot in flowery dresses,
Running up and down the sidewalk,
Carrying play-purses and dollies.
Their mom always stops the ice cream man when he comes—
Always buys them "Sidewalk Sundaes."

Two houses up from here is Mister Gumm's house.
There is no white sidewalk in front of his house.
He is the only neighbor on Mavis without one.
He wants no one walking through his ivy garden.
But people walk through the ivy anyway.
I see them all the time.
There's a little dirt path there now.
The Missus says Mister Gumm is fit to be tied about it.

I see him come home at nights driving a Hostess cupcake truck.
Me and Dennis Nelson chase the truck down his driveway a lot—
We yell for Mister Gumm before he disappears.
"Hey Mister Gumm! Got any leftovers?"
Most of the time, he says no.
He's never in a good mood.
But one time a miracle happened.
I think it was Christmas time.
Dennis Nelson got two snowballs.
I like the chocolate cupcakes better.
Never got any of those.

These elm trees are high.
In summertime, they are shady and cool.
I like to wait in the shade for the ice cream man.
Sometimes I can hear him coming five streets away.
He sounds like a loud carousel coming from Disneyland.
I can hear him on Mesagrove, then Ben Alder and Adele.
I wonder if I'll get a Free Stick today?

3
"NO NEED TO LOOK INSIDE THERE"

This is my house.
I live at 817 Mavis, in this beige house.
Here, you never go in through the front door.
You always go in where my mom says to go in—
The back door.
This is the door that leads into our little kitchen.
Look, there's my mom making dinner at the gas stove.
She is a big woman. A loud and friendly woman.
She is frying hamburger patties with a blue dress on.
The Mister likes to see my mom in a dress.
She wears one all the time, from morning to bedtime.

Now we step past the stove and into the little dining area…
I see my mom's dining table and tea cart.
I like the curtains she has covering the windows.
I can look outside a lot and no one knows it.
I can hide behind them and watch Life go by.

The TV in the corner of the living room is a few years old.
The gray sofa looks old but isn't.
I like my mom's two end tables with the bubble lamps.
I sit in this room a lot,..
Watching TV, and eating TV dinners on a TV tray.
My mom always tells me to not sit close to the TV as I eat.

Come with me down the hallway now…

My room is first on the left.
I have two windows and book shelves.
This is the door to my closet.
Open it.
Yes, just what you might expect, clothes and toys.
All my baseball cards are inside this closet.
Across the hallway is the bathroom—
Bathtub, sink and toilet. And a mirror.
I like to look at myself in the mirror a lot.
I don't think I am ugly at all,
Not like what some of the kids have said.
I can see my two front teeth sticking out a little, like a chipmunk's.
But I am not ugly.

There are two more bedrooms.
They're at the end of the hallway—
My brother's room with his bed and dresser.
There is a portable radio constantly playing inside his room.
Underneath his bed, hidden from my mom, are his Playboys.
They're hard to see because his Hot Rods are there too.
I look at his Playboys when no is home.
I like to see naked women.
It makes my heart beat more when I do.
And across from my brother's room is my parent's room,
With a big King-sized bed—
A clothes bureau and a dressing table with a large mirror.
On a bedside table is a zenith radio with a ticking clock.
Their closet is filled with clothes, shoes, and blue luggage…
No need to look inside there…

4
"I LIKE BLONDE KIDS"

I like my street.
The ice cream man comes down this street.
He has blonde hair and is nice to me.
The Helms Man comes up this street.
He is nice to me too, but he isn't blonde.
Everyday they visit, and everyday they stop.
Dennis Nelson buys a crumb donut every Saturday.
Erik Nelson does the same but prefers the jelly-filled glazed ones.
They never buy donuts for their sisters.

Look.
Watch Dennis Nelson run with the donut to his backyard,
And hide there.
He's eating that donut like a hungry bear.
I like Dennis Nelson.
He is a honest boy who is not afraid of the big kids.
But that doesn't mean he is all brave.
He once told me he's afraid of German Shepard dogs.
He hates those dogs because he was attacked by one when he was small.
Don't blame him really.

There's Clint Tiernan riding his 10-Speed with no hands.
He lives over on Adele by Patty Miller's house.
He cruises down this street every day about this time.
I think he likes Wanda Stultz and is just showing off.

Across the street I can see the Koontz family—
Leaving in their red and black-finned station wagon.
The Mister is driving. He is a quiet man, like my dad.
The Missus is in the front seat too.
She has short blonde hair and wears tight dresses to work.
They have two kids,
A teenage daughter named Kristy, and a boy named Randy.
I like them.
They don't tell me to go away when I go there to play.
Kristy likes to suntan in a bikini bathing suit in her backyard.
For a kid, she has a big chest.
Randy likes to play catch with his football.
He puts on his helmet and shoulder pads to play catch with his dad.
They play on their front yard.
Sometimes the Missus suntans with Kristy in the backyard.
They have lounges and tiki torches back there.
They lie there a long time and laugh a lot.
Both Randy and his sister are blondes.
I like blonde kids. They are nice to me.

5
"I LIKE LIVING ON MAVIS STREET"

Four houses up from the Koontz house is the Stultz house.
I like the Stultzes.
The Mister is a big man who works at Alcoa Aluminum.
He dropped bombs from a B-17 during the war.
The Missus is a nice lady with long black hair.
Most of the time she sits in her house wearing a faded bathing suit,
And smoking cigarettes, I have seen her.
She plays records real loud.
Her favorite is Dave "Baby" Cortez playing the "Happy Organ."
I like that song. It makes me happy.
It makes the Missus happy.
But I don't think she is happy.
Sometimes I hear her weeping in the kitchen.
Sometimes I see her dancing by herself in their tiny living room…
She in that swimsuit that barely covers her private parts.
I've seen her black hair down there as she lies on her couch,
Reading and smoking Chesterfields.
She doesn't care one bit about it either.

They have five kids living in that tiny house.
I hear a lot of yelling going on sometimes inside there.
There's Wanda, the oldest at 15; she has long blond hair.
Next is Glenn, who is one year younger;
Then there are the twins, Kathy and Kenny, who are 12,
And the youngest, Larry. I think he's 10.
These kids are all fun to play with.

Wanda is in love with Elvis.
She plays "Return To Sender" about a million times a day.
I like the Stultzes.
Kenny and Kathy like to share their cookies with me…

My mom won't let me play with Glenn Stultz anymore.
It's been three years since he showed the guys that war picture;
The one he found in his father's cedar chest—
That German soldier with his face crushed in by a sledgehammer.
Me and Larry Stultz cried when we saw it because it was awful—
Never want to see anything like that again.
The Missus got angry about it when she found out.
She told Glenn Stultz to stay away from me for now on.
He did.

…See that white house?
Up there, by the brown picket fence?
That red and white Ford station wagon belongs to the Robertson Family.
The Mister drives the Ford.
He wears a tie to work.
Sometimes I see Mister Robertson upset when he comes home.
The Missus is a nice lady named Hope.
They have four kids; some big, some little…
There's Greg, Leigh, Randy and… I don't remember the baby's name.
Randy Robertson is my age.
He is my friend.
I like him because he has a lot of baseball cards in his room.
Sometimes he gives cards away for free.
I want a Duke Snider card.
One time Mister Robertson took Randy and the guys to the El Mercado.

He bought us all baseball cards.
Then he treated us to milk shakes at the Beverly Fountain.
I like Mister Robertson.
Going home now…
The sun is setting beyond the school yard.
It is a bright orange color as usual…
If you look way over there,
You can see the power lines snaking their way to LA.
If you sit on your front yard for a long time,
You'll hear the big Constellations flying by —up in the sky,
Heading west to the airport.
It's been another smoggy day today.
My chest hurts bad from all the smoke in the air.
But I have gotten used to it.

I like living on Mavis Street.

6
"AS MISSUS SABATINI SMILES"

I play radio station KRLA on my clock radio everyday.
I keep it next to my bed.
All my friends listen to KRLA, except the Nelsons.
Missus Nelson hates rock and roll music.
She says it is part of a Communist plot.
Her Catholic children are forbidden to listen to Elvis, Fabian and
Chubby Checker—
Or any song on KRLA.
Even Lawrence Welk.
I think it's dumb.

Let's go into the kitchen now…
There's my mom cooking at the white gas range,
Wearing a blue dress again.
She's making bacon and eggs for the Mister.
I like Saturdays—
Especially the mornings when you can smell breakfast all over the house.
You just know the day will be a good one.
There's no school and I can stay home and play outside with my friends.
I like my friends.
I pour maple syrup on my bacon as I sit at the kitchen table.
The Missus tells me to go outside when finished with breakfast.
I will, after I look at my baseball cards for awhile.
I stare at the Cleveland Indians team card of 1955.
I can see Bob Feller sitting there. And Gene Woodling too.

Going outside now through the back door…
Across the street I see the crazy Jeffy Sabatini—
Sitting inside his dad's pickup truck.
He's pretending to drive it.
The guys laugh at him all the time.

Now he's running down the sidewalk like a nut—
Playing army with Scotty, his little brother.
He wants all the kids to play with them.
But Jeffy Sabatini doesn't follow the rules.
He won't play dead when we play army.
So no kids play with them.
I don't like to play with Jeffy Sabatini.
I don't like to play with any kid who won't be the dead Jap.

Now little Scotty is pounding a toy drum.
Here comes Missus Sabatini to get little Scotty and his drum.
I like the Missus.
She's pretty with big eyes and long legs.
She is nice to me too.
Once she stopped the ice cream man,
And bought all the guys popsicles…

Now the Nelsons are driving down Mavis in their Rambler station wagon.
Missus Nelson is driving this time,
With little Tina next to her on the front seat.
Valerie and Kathleen sit in the back seat with their windows open.
I can see their red hair waving in the fast wind…
Now I hear KRLA playing inside Missus Sabatini's little kitchen window.
The Tymes are singing "So Much In Love" as Missus Sabatini smiles…

7
"I LIKE TO PLAY ARMY"

Living next door to the Sabatini's is the Hope family.
They came to Mavis from Joplin, Missouri;
The Mister and the Missus are the nicest people on the street—
They and their 4 kids, Ronnie, Stevie, Patty and baby Sherry,
Live in the middle of the block.
My brother likes the Hopes.
He plays with Stevie everyday.
They ride bikes to Palm Park in the afternoons.
They swim in the big pool there.

Once my brother had his bike stolen.
The police came to our house to take a report,
But my brother never got his bike back.
I liked his bike.
It had goose-neck handlebars and
Monster decals on the frame.
It was wicked.

I hear voices inside their garage…
Let's go up their driveway to see what the Hopes are doing.
The Missus is laughing out loud at the Mister over a pitcher of lemonade.
He says it's too sweet, like her.
The Mister is wearing black-framed glasses and dirty coveralls.
He likes to work on old cars with Ronnie and Stevie helping him.
They have a radio playing in the garage,
Hooked up to two loudspeakers…

Now I hear Donnie Brooke singing "Mission Bell" on KRLA.
Mister Hope is telling Ronnie and Stevie to clean up the garage.
Missus Hope comes outside again,
Bringing more lemonade.
She is a blond woman who speaks with a Missouri accent.
The Mister hugs her as he drinks the new lemonade.

I see Dennis Nelson coming out of his back door—
Directly across the street.
He's peeling a big orange.
Sometimes I feel bad for Dennis.
He's a fat kid with a million freckles on his face.
But the big kids don't pick on him.
That's why I like him.
He likes to eat at the Beverly Fountain, so once
Him and me and Kenny Stultz went there.
He likes french fries and ice cream.

Now Dennis Nelson is eating a huge orange.
He eats it like a badger in the woods.
He says he wants to play army.
I'll play army anytime with the guys.
But I do not like to play the dead Jap.
But if no one else wants to, I will.
We let Jeffy Sabatini play with us once in a while.
But he has to be the Jap, and die.
I like to play army.

8
"MAYBE MISTER GUMM HAS EXTRAS"

I can hear my brother's record player…
I can hear him playing it way down here, at the Stultzes.
His bedroom window is wide open today because it's hot.
He's playing his 45's on a stackable 45 record player,
That plays real loud.
He plays Elvis, Pat Boone, Dickie Doo and the Don'ts,
Jimmy Dorsey.
That's who he's playing now…
Listen.
It's "So Rare" by Jimmy Dorsey on a 45.
I like "So Rare."
It sounds good to my ears.
It reminds me of summertime and ice cream.

Larry Stultz is a little kid with buck teeth.
But I like him because he is fun to play with.
The guys want to play army today but he says no.
He says he wants to play "Monster."
I like to play Monster.
No one has to die when we play Monster,
And the best part is,
Dennis Nelson plays the monster.
He likes to chase us, growling like a gorilla,
Around and around the house, and
We run and scream for our lives.
Dennis Nelson is the scariest monster on our street.

The best place to hide,
When playing Monster is my mom's bedroom…

Dennis Nelson will never find me here.
My parents' bedroom is off-limits;
It is beige-walled and crowded with a big bed.
Though my dad sleeps here, it is really my mom's room.
Here she puts on a lot of make-up to her face,
As she looks at herself in the big mirror.
When she puts on red lipstick, she puts it on thickly—
Then uses a tissue to remove the extra red paste from her lips.
The Missus is pretty with big blue eyes.
Her legs are big too.
But the Missus is fat in her stomach.

Many times I've seen her put on that white girdle of hers…
Sweating and struggling like crazy,
Just to pull that ugly thing up and over her big hips.
It's like watching something awful get born.
Now days I get embarrassed around my friends when she comes out.
That's a bad thing to say, but it's true…

Hiding here in my mom's room is getting boring…
All I can hear is the clock radio ticking…

I will go back outside now.
I can see Larry Stultz hiding behind the front yard tree.
Here comes the Monster, Dennis Nelson,
Our orange-eating friend,
Growling like something we all have seen on Saturday morning television.

Kenny Stultz runs down Mavis Street now,
Looking for a shady spot to escape to, from
This fat-freckled thing from Boston, Massachusetts.

Now I join Larry by the tall elm tree, and I see him crying.
I don't understand until I see why.
Larry Stultz has peed in his blue shorts.
I tell him it's okay. No one will notice.
Larry Stultz stops crying…
There is a smile covering his buck teeth.
But now, the monster runs up and bear-hugs Larry Stultz.
He growls something awful, something even worse,
When the boy, Dennis Nelson, sees Larry's pee,
Smeared on his Catholic school trousers.

The sun is setting now…
I see Miss Jane sitting on her front porch.
She's smoking a cigarette with her husband.
I can hear Johnny Ray singing inside her house—
"Walking My Baby Back Home"…
My mom loves that record.
Miss Jane waves for me and Dennis Nelson to come over.
We walk across the street as the music gets louder…
She says she loves Johnny Ray and has all his records.
I tell her I like this song a lot.
Miss Jane says it's her favorite.
Again she puffs on her cigarette and blows out the smoke…

The sun now looks like a big orange beachball.
The smog was bad today.

The guys were coughing a lot.
Time for me to go home.
Time now for the guys to go home too,
And time now to watch Popeye on Channel 5.

Our mothers are cooking dinner in their small kitchens.
Our fathers will soon be coming home from work—
Driving their Falcons, Fairlanes, and Comets—
Maybe Mister Gumm has extras.

9
"I REALLY DON'T GET IT"

Dennis Nelson is eating another orange.
This one is even bigger than the last one.
We're sitting on the Wooster front yard—
Talking about which kids on the street are the spoiled kids.
Dennis Nelson thinks he's not spoiled.
He is talking loudly now about his strict parents and his big family.
He says they are Catholics, and
His dad always gives ten percent of his Sears paycheck to the church.
He is saying that's why they are poor.
It all goes to God.
I think that's a good Catholic thing to do.
To be poor for God.

Now Dennis Nelson calls out the names—
Of those he considers "spoiled rotten to the core."
Randy Koontz has a color TV set in his house.
He's spoiled.
The Wooster Brothers all have new bikes and new baseball gloves.
They're spoiled.
Eddie Magehee has two train sets running all the time in his garage.
He's spoiled.
And now finally,
Dennis Nelson, my protector and friend, is telling me
I'm spoiled.
He says I have my own room, and
My mom let's me listen to KRLA.

He's right.
I'm spoiled.

Now we see Shirley Sisson,
Coming out of her house with her boyfriend.
She has a very high hair-do;
It's like Mister Sisson's hair—
It spirals upward like a big beehive, and
Could easily be used as a soft nest by any bird.
I would like to be a bird in Shirley Sisson's nest.
She's a pretty girl with a big chest.
I like big chests.

Her boyfriend has short red hair,
Cut evenly in a flat-top style.
He wears black glasses, and
Me and the guys know he doesn't like us.
I don't like him at all.
When he drives Shirley away on one of their dates,
He revs his car real loud, and off he goes
Down the street with smoke coming out of it.

Today Dennis Nelson tells us to watch him.
Kenny and Larry stand up to watch, and so do I.
There they go now,
Shirley Sisson and her boyfriend,
Again dragging that black and red Studebaker…
Down Mavis street roaring real loud!
Now Dennis Nelson is running down Mavis Street too,
Yelling, "Hey Rover!"

We guys are falling on the grass now,
Laughing at the name "Rover." Except,
I don't get it.
I'm laughing with the guys like crazy, but
I really don't get it.

10
"I DON'T THINK THAT'S TRUE AT ALL"

Here comes Missus Wooster.
Mother to Stevie, Robbie and Gary.
I like Stevie, Robbie and Gary Wooster because they share their toys, and
Because Missus Wooster looks like a movie star.
She looks like Marilyn Monroe, but with dark curly hair instead.
Missus Wooster has a small chest.
I like women with small chests and with big chests.
Kenny Stultz's mom has a small chest, and
I like her because she gives cookies to the guys.

Missus Wooster is mad at us.
She wants us to get off her nice lawn… now.
She says she works hard on her lawn, and
Doesn't want us playing on it.
Dennis Nelson gets up first.
He says we guys are just talking.
The Missus says No, and she doesn't mean maybe.

I like Missus Wooster.
She doesn't have a big chest, but
She does have a big heart.
She is changing her mind now.
She tells us we can stay where we are,
As long as we don't run around on it.
Now she is wondering what time it is.

She is walking back to the house.
I watch her.

Missus Wooster's legs are slender and tan,
With little worms of muscle sticking out.
I look at her green lawn and I can see that it is neat, like her.
I have seen Missus Wooster mowing it with my own two eyes—
From across the street…
I have seen her trimming the bushes and flowers for a long time.
I watch her from behind my mom's curtain in the dining room.
I can see everything that is going on from there.
Sometimes I think it is a mortal sin to spy.
If not that, then it's at least a venial sin.

My mom is coming out now—
Through the back door with her white apron on.
She is calling for me to come over to her.
She has fifty cents in her hand for crumb donuts.
Soon the Helms donut man will be honking.
I like the Helms man.
His truck smells good.

My mom sees Missus Wooster now, and crosses the street.
They are saying hello to each other and laughing.
My mom says she likes Missus Wooster's new hairdo.
They are talking about Kennedy now, and
Whether there will be war soon.
My mom hopes not,
And says she doesn't dwell on it much.
Missus Wooster now wonders what my mom is making for dinner tonight.

My mom laughs and says she hasn't decided.
But that she would soon be going to the Model.

I like the Model Market.
It has toys, 45's, candy and orange drinks.
My mom likes the meat. Manning's Beef.
All the ladies of Mavis Street shop there wearing jewelry.
All the misters buy their scotch and beer there.
I have even seen misters with mustaches at the Model.
My mom thinks men with mustaches are sinners—
At least they certainly are not Catholics…
I don't think that's true at all.

INTERMISSION 1

THE AUTHOR IS READY TO GO TO CATHOLIC SCHOOL.
PICTURED IS THE TOY-LADEN FRONT YARD ON MAVIS STREET. THE SUN IS RISING IN 1958. THE SILVER CONSTELLATIONS ARE FLYING.

11
"I LIKE TWINKIES"

Next door to the Nelsons lives Mrs. Correll.
She's a widow who lives by herself in that gray house.
I only see her when she comes out to water her lawn.
Dennis Nelson says she's a teacher, and
Gives out good candy at Halloween.
Far as I can tell no one talks to her or even visits her.
I never see any relatives or friends.
She keeps her windows closed most of the time,
But once I saw her looking out her window.
I wonder what she does inside her house, what she thinks.
I like Mrs. Correll.
I see her now outside watering the grass.
She is old-looking and wears glasses.
But she's nice to us.

Here comes Mister Gumm driving his truck up Mavis Street…
Dennis Nelson hears the rumbling cupcake truck and
Runs as fast as he can to catch up,
Before Mister Gumm disappears deeply into his back yard.
I can hear him begging now…
"Mister Gumm! Any leftovers?"

Now I see my friend
Coming back down the street to his house.
He is wearing his Cub Scout tee-shirt.
I ask him if he got any leftovers.

Dennis Nelson says nothing as he walks by us—
The guys —his friends in the Tree Top Club—
We keep watching him, seeing what he's up to…

Now I am spying for the Tree Top Club…
I am on patrol to find out what Dennis Nelson is doing.
I am following him now into his back yard.
But he can't see me.
What I see is a back yard of green crabgrass with a rusty swing set.
But behind the garage there, I see my friend and protector,
Again, secretly biting into two Twinkies like a hungry bear.
Dennis Nelson truly is a monster!

I like Twinkies.

12
"KENNY STULTZ IS LAUGHING NOW"

The guys are in the front yard on bikes.
There's Kenny and Larry Stultz on their beaten-up Sting-Rays.
The Wooster Brothers, Stevie and Robbie, are aboard their new Racers.
Randy Koontz is there on his scratched-up Huffy.
Dennis Nelson is on his brother's old bike.
Not sure what that is. Probably an old Jaguar.

They are telling me to get on my bike and follow them.
They're riding down to Orange Grove to play bike tag.
Dennis Nelson says he found a small beanbag in his bedroom;
Says it's perfect for throwing at some kid.
So now I run to the garage to get my bike…

This garage is filled with my mom's new furniture,
Covered like cookies and pies with saran-wrap,
Waiting here in all this dust for a new home.
My bike is in the back with a blue tarp over it—
A 1961 Schwinn three-speed Racer with silver headlamp.

I don't like my bike. It's too high for me.
When I stop, I almost fall off. It's too hard to balance.
But once I get my balance, I can ride it fast like the Woosters.
I like a small bike.
I like it because I can ride it with no hands.

The Orange Grove School grounds are big and green.

There are three swing sets, a merry-go-round and a sandbox.
And many shady trees are here too.
The guys like to park their bikes under the big tree,
Over there, by the picnic tables.
Dennis Nelson now tells us to sit on the grass and cool down.
He thinks it's hot.
And now he wishes for an orange drink from the Model.

Larry Stultz says a train is coming.
He's right. I can feel the ground grumbling now.
The orange freighter that comes by here,
On the other side of that fence out there,
Is loud as it buckles along like a big steel bug.
But I like trains.
Now Dennis Nelson says let's race to the tracks.
I get on my bike first and am going as fast as I can.
I am just flying across the green grass like Sky King.
But Kenny Stultz beats me to the fence on his sting-ray.
He waves to the train engineer, who waves back.
I tell him he cheated because his bike is small.
Kenny Stultz is laughing now.

13
"DENNIS NELSON HATES STEW"

I like my treehouse.
The guys in the Tree Top Club helped build it.
Dennis Nelson brought the wood and the hammer.
Kenny Stultz brought the blankets and the rope.
Larry Stultz brought the nails and the Milk Duds.

There are days like today when I sit up here,
Under these orange branches and think.
I like to think.
I think about school,
And why the Sisters are mean sometimes.
I think about God, and Mass on Sundays.
Sometimes I think about big kids picking on little kids.
Mostly I think about baseball cards and candy.

I am now climbing up to the highest point—
Way way up there at the peak of this thorny tree.
I'll be okay. I am a good climber.
Now I am stretching up on tip-toe as high as I can.
This cross-branch is strong enough to hold me.
Look. I can see the sandbox at Orange Grove.
I can even see the railroad tracks,
Way, way over there by the chain-link fence—
Way beyond all these houses and their green lawns.
Truly, no one can see what I can see up here…

All the guys went home after the train passed.
All except me and Dennis Nelson...

We are still riding bikes here at Orange Grove,
Still watching the Constellations fly overhead to LA.
It is always quiet here as the afternoon tires out.
But you can always hear other kids—
Playing late games of Hopscotch in the distance.
Now Dennis Nelson says he is starving.
He wonders what his mom is making tonight for dinner.
He loves tuna fish casserole with white crackers.
He hates chicken livers, stew and fried spam.
Now we begin to walk our bikes across this big yard—
This living ocean of grass that has no fish...

Inside the Nelson house now.
Dennis Nelson is washing his face—
Scrubbing gently with Boraxo soap.
I am with him in his little beige bathroom,
Looking at the 20 Mule Team on the black can.
I like Death Valley Days on TV.
The Old Ranger reminds me of God talking.

Missus Nelson is fixing dinner in her small kitchen.
I can see a bloody crucifix on the wall.
Jesus Christ is dying there as she cooks meat.
The Missus is wearing a dress and black shoes.
Her flaming hair-do reminds me of a round red pillow.
All eight Nelsons will soon be sitting in this kitchen,
Sitting at two tables shoved together by the Mister,

Eating another Catholic meal wearing clean clothes.
Now I recognize it—
The smell of Missus Nelson's dinner tonight…
Dennis Nelson hates stew.

14
"GOD HAS LEFT THE BUILDING"

I like Mass.
I like the smells in here…
When I'm kneeling in the pew, I feel clean inside;
I feel like God is happy with me today.
I pray the "Our Father" on my knees.
Then I get up and sit on the bench.
I feel real relieved when I'm done.
Maybe Jesus will be punching my heavenly ticket again.
Maybe he's putting my name on his Saint's List right now…

Father Elliot is my favorite priest at this church.
When he says High Mass, he sings better than the others.
Father Dawson is a good singer too.
He can sing the high notes without cracking his voice.
Fathers Dowd and Aggler sound off-key most of the time.
Father Heidker cannot sing at all.

Today's Mass is being said in Latin by Father Elliot.
The four altar boys up there are 8th graders.
I think when they answer the priest during Mass,
They are faking the Latin.
Sometimes they mess up the bell-ringing too.
The holiest part is when the priest lifts the Host—
Way up high at the altar.
You have to be able to ring the holy bells right on time.
Otherwise the miracle of the Host doesn't work…

Now I am in line for Holy Communion.
Everyone at Mass today is in line it seems.
Soon I will be at the communion rail…

Kneeling here I know I am very close to God…
At least I am close to him on that big crucifix over there…
The altar is big and shiny—
Perfect size for an animal sacrifice.
Here comes my favorite priest with the little Host.
He speaks Latin.
And now, I open my mouth to receive Christ's body…
I like eating the Host.
It tastes good, like dry bread.
Sometimes it sticks to the roof of my mouth.

Returning now to my pew in back,
I notice all these Catholics kneeling in deep prayer.
Some have their heads down, covering their faces.
They must all be ashamed of something.
Or afraid.

I am kneeling too now.
After awhile my knees start to get tired.
So I like to look at all the stained glass windows.
They help me to feel close to God.
This church must be something like heaven itself.
Now I hear the organ playing in the choir loft.
It is time for the Benediction…
Father Molthen is up there.
He is playing the organ like Dave Baby Cortez.

As he plays, he moves his head and shoulders…

Father Elliot extends the final blessing to us all.
I like this part because we can all relax now.
We Catholics can get off our knees finally.
God has left the building…

15
"THE MISSUS FINDS A SURPRISE"

Sunday morning now at the Hadley Car Wash.
The Mister is driving the '58 Impala to the entrance.
He does this every week after Mass.
KRLA is playing Elvis on the radio—
"Good Luck Charm."

At the entrance there are long vacuum hoses.
A negro lady wearing a baseball cap,
Has a clip-board and a coin-changer.
She smiles at my dad.
The Mister knows this lady, I can tell.
There are other negroes working here.
They are nice and work hard.

Now the car is getting cleaned with soap.
The man cleaning my dad's white walls is very black.
Black as Jackie Robinson on my baseball card.
I wave to him as I watch.
He waves back.
I like Negroes.
They are nice to me and my dad.
I can hear music now coming from a loudspeaker.
It sounds like the Diamonds.
"Little Darlin'" is filling the air now with their singing voices.
Are the Diamonds negroes?
I wonder…

Come on. Get in the car.
We're going home now.
This '58 Impala smells good inside.
My place is in the backseat, behind my dad.
You can sit with me behind my mom.
Here we go…

The way back home is confusing.
Luckily the Mister knows how.
He is reaching for a Pall Mall as he slows.
He lights it with the car's cigarette lighter.
The light turns green.
He exhales a cloud of smoke.
Let's see, this is Magnolia. He's turning left.

Good, I like this song.
I tell my mom to turn up the radio.
KRLA is playing "Norman" by Sue Thompson.
Now we're coming to a stop at Beverly.
Today is a good day.
The Missus is happy and smoking a Salem.
I like sunny days riding in the Impala.
I like it when my parents smoke and talk.
That is when I know they like each other.
Now we're driving on Beverly Boulevard,
Going under all these tall pine trees.
They stand like green giants on both sides of Beverly—
Way higher than telephone poles.
It's like riding in a magic tunnel to heaven…

The Missus tells the Mister she needs to go to the Model.
She needs bread, milk, liverwurst, and cokes.
The Mister now signals to turn left at Norwalk Boulevard.
We are stopped at a red light, watching the cross-traffic pass by.
I see a lot of church people eating inside the Beverly Fountain.
I like Jack's Beverly Fountain.
The spaghetti is good there…

The Missus exhales a cloud of smoke now from her Salem.
She tells the Mister to also get some Wampum and Hostess.
Now my dad turns into the back entrance of the Model,
Then turns right again behind the store—
Circling finally into the front parking lot.
The Mister parks the Impala by the long ramp.
There are many cars parked here today.
Church people are shopping for the week's groceries.
They are going up and down the cement ramp,
Dressed in their best Sunday clothes.
All the ladies are wearing white and blue hats.

Look. There's Missus Robertson coming down the ramp.
Box-boy, Ronnie Hope, is right behind her,
Carrying bags of groceries to her station wagon.
My dad is coming out now with a smile on his face.
He's carrying two bags and a six-pack of Coke.
He gets in and gives the bags to the Missus.
He gives the cokes to me.
Now he lights another Pall Mall.
As he exhales another white cloud of smoke,
The Missus finds a surprise…

16
"LARRY STULTZ CANNOT BELIEVE HIS EYES"

Randy Robertson is riding fast today.
Me and the guys can see him gliding down Mavis,
Flying like a jet, on his new 10 speed Continental.
It's wicked.
He's showing it off now,
Riding it up and down the street like Clint Tiernan.
Sometimes he's standing up using the pedals,
Riding high without hands so the guys can see him.
And we do see him, the Luck-out.
The guys are here at my house for a club meeting.
But now here comes Randy Robertson to talk.
He stops at the curbside and says hi.
We say hello back pretending not to see his bike.

Now he asks if we guys have seen it yet?
Dennis Nelson speaks first as always.
He asks the Luck-out kid, "Seen what"?
Now Randy Robertson smiles and laughs.
He says it's at Orange Grove School—
Something scary and gross—
Under the big tree by the merry-go-round.
He says it's wicked and we gotta see it.
Dennis Nelson says we'll go down there on bikes,
But not until tomorrow.
He says his chest hurts from the smog.
The guys agree with Dennis Nelson as usual.

Now Randy Koontz speaks up.
He says we should all go to the Nelson House to play.
But Dennis Nelson says no.
The guys can't go to his house because of his three little sisters.
I don't understand…

The Tree Top Club is meeting—
High up in our tree house now.
We are sitting on strong branches under old blankets.
Dennis Nelson is here, eating another big orange.
He says all members need to meet here tomorrow after school's out.
He also says if any member is too scared to go see it,
That is fine. They don't have to go.
Kenny Stultz says tomorrow might be too late to go see it.
School is on, and the teachers might get rid of it first.
Dennis Nelson agrees.
Whatever is down at Orange Grove, we must go see it now…

Entering inside my house now.
My mom is at the white stove making dinner.
She is wearing a navy-blue dress.
It smells like goulash tonight.
I like goulash.
I ask her if I can go down to Orange Grove with the guys.
She says for only a half hour, and
To not snack on anything before dinner.
Now I notice on the counter her own half-eaten snack.
I ask her how she got the giant Hershey bar.
She says to never mind about the Hershey bar.
If was just a sweet surprise from my father,

From when we went to the Model yesterday.
The Missus is fat.
So, why does the Mister keep buying her fatty snacks?

Now the members of the Tree Top Club are riding—
Riding down Mavis Street like cowboys going after outlaws.
Kenny Stultz is the leader of our pack.
Come on, he yells.
One by one in single file,
The guys ride down the dirt path into the school yard.
The sun is beginning to go down now.
Overhead, I can hear a constellation flying to LA.
Man, that thing is loud!
Now the guys get to the big tree by the merry-go-round.
Kenny Stultz jumps off his sting-ray pointing.
He yells to look at that!
Larry Stultz cannot believe his eyes.

17
"AS YOUNG AS SHIRLEY SISSON AND ROVER"

I cannot eat this.
My mom's goulash looks gross to me.
Not sure what's in it.
It smells alright I guess.
It has meat, corn, cheese, tomato sauce, onions.
But it reminds me of… It.

When the guys all got to the big tree at Orange Grove,
What we saw was really gross.
I remember thinking it was the Blob from outer space.
It was a red smelly pile of barf.
That's what Kenny Stultz said, and
Dennis Nelson said he thought it was barf too.
Thinking back on it,
I don't think Larry Stultz had ever seen barf before.
He looked sick to his stomach.
Randy Koontz found a stick and decided to stab the barf.
Then Larry found one.
He started doing the same thing.
Before you know it,
All the guys were stabbing the barf.
That was wicked…

I like my mom's cooking.
But tonight I don't.
Her goulash looks like the barf.

The Missus wants to know why I'm not eating.
She says her goulash is delicious.
I tell her I am not feeling good—
That my stomach hurts.
Now she is feeling my forehead.
I can tell she is confused.
Too bad I don't have a fever.
Then I would have a good excuse,
For not eating my mom's delicious goulash.

It's 8:30.
This is my bedtime.
The Missus is very strict with this rule.
No one argues with my mom.
Not even the Mister…

I like my room.
I have two windows.
In the mornings when I wake up,
I like to look out my second window…
As I lie there, I can see the house next door.
I can see the newlywed couple inside their kitchen,
Sitting at a small table across from each other.
The wife has dark brown hair up in a bun.
The husband is blonde with tan skin.
They don't seem to talk much—
Just sit there eating their breakfast in silence.
They look real young,
As young as Shirley Sisson and Rover.

18
"I LIKE LIVERWURST"

There they are.
It's Shirley and Rover.
Parked in front of our house.
It's 5:45 in the morning.
And they are kissing in Rover's car.
No one is up yet,
So there they are, necking like crazy,
Thinking it's too early for someone to see them.
But here I am, hiding behind the curtains.
I can see Shirley Sisson kissing Rover's mouth,
Like she's trying to get his gum.
Wait a second…
Now Shirley is gone.
She disappeared.
Rover is sitting back behind the steering wheel,
Like he's sleeping.
Where did Shirley go?
Oh, okay. There she is.
She has her head on his lap, sleeping.
It must be a tiring thing to kiss so much.

I hope school today isn't boring.
Sister Maria is my teacher.
She wears glasses and has puffy cheeks.
I like her because she likes me.
She actually thinks I'm smart.

Never heard that before.
The Mister calls me "dummy-head."
The Missus can't understand why I'm "so dense."
If only I had a dime for every time I was called stupid.

My desk in Room 12 is by the window.
Robert Murphy sits in front of me.
He likes "Surfin USA" by The Beach Boys.
Sitting behind me is big Jeff Muller.
He likes to pile all his supplies on top of his desk.
Once a day I topple all his stuff to the floor with my swinging elbow.
He never gets mad at me.
I like Jeff Muller.

Father Molthen is teaching us classical music today.
Once a week during lunch he gets on the intercom.
He has a record player set up in the Principal's office.
We all have to sit in our classrooms and listen to this stuff.
Actually, I like some of it, like Bach.
Today he going on about Beethoven.
I don't pay attention to him.
He is reading to us from a book.
That's boring.
Now he's playing Symphony Number 5.
Over at the door stands Miss "Shone Bones."
She's watching two classrooms as Sister eats lunch.
Now she's telling Timmy McGann to sit down.
Up front in row one, I see Gary Casanova.
He's flirting with Cindy Stevens.
I hope those two will be very happy.

Patty Miller is the prettiest girl in class.
She sits in the first desk of this row.
Her blonde hair looks friendly to me.
It reminds me of a waterfall of white fire.
Her legs are strong and tan; everyday
She rides her Schwinn Spitfire all the way to school,
Then rides all the way back home to Adele street.

Finally this symphony is finished.
The Missus made a liverwurst sandwich today.
I like liverwurst.

19
"I LIKE MISS JANE"

Kenny Stultz is knocking on my back door.
It is now 4 o'clock, and I can play.
He has Randy Robertson's Flexy Flyer.
For Christmas last year I got one too.
His idea is to hook the two flyers together.
Then with me steering in front,
And he doing the hard pushing in the rear,
We hoped to travel the entire length of Mavis—
Starting up at Beverly Boulevard,
Then coasting all the way down,
To Orange Grove Street.
We both agreed that would be wicked.

Now we're taking our Flexies up to Kenny's house.
He wants to get Larry to ride with us.
Here comes Larry Stultz.
He has his Dodger tee-shirt on today.
He's excited to ride. Hurry he says.

Today is a hot day.
The afternoon is sweltering now.
The street is crowded with neighbors outside.
Listen.
"Wild Weekend" is playing on someone's radio.
I can't tell the guys what I'm thinking.
Can't tell them, that now, is the best time of my life.

WHITE SIDEWALKS

We are now ready to ride our Flexy Fliers.
Kenny has placed mine half-way on top of Randy's,
Giving us six wheels instead of four.
Larry is in front, I'm in the middle and Kenny is in the back.
The sidewalk before us is a straight white line.
I can see Orange Grove way down there.
This afternoon is alive with children yelling.
I am having so much fun.

Now Kenny Stultz is pushing us down the sidewalk.
Passing a lot of green lawns and front-yard trees,
Passing a lot of mothers with kids pointing.
Now we are coming to the Armstrongs and the Mooney's.
Passing the Ghans' and the Myers' houses.
There's Clint Tiernan now riding with no hands,
Smiling big, passing us by on his 10-Speed.
Little boys now are following us as we ride.
Kenny is pushing us again as we go faster.
Passing now the Gumm and the Bliss houses,
Past the Hope, Carrell and Nelson houses…

There's my mom coming out now with Missus Koontz.
They are smoking my mom's Salems on the front lawn.
They are talking loudly in knee-length dresses,
Something about Kennedy and Khrushchev.
Miss Jane is outside too, smoking on her front porch.
I can hear a Johnny Ray record playing inside her house.
She tells us to come down the sidewalk again.
This time, she says, her Rain-Birds will be spraying.

Mavis street is busy now with twilight voices.
Yet, I see no misters outside, only the moms.
And what seems to be hundreds of screaming kids.
I want to tell Larry something.
I want to tell him life is real wicked right now…

Again we are flying down the white sidewalk.
Again, all the mothers on their lawns are pointing,
All the little kids are running with us.
Here comes Miss Jane's house again.
With Kenny pushing hard,
We smoothly swish by on her wet sidewalk,
Feeling the cool spray of her Rain-Bird sprinklers…
Miss Jane is running in the water by us, laughing.
She and the moms are clapping their hands loudly,
As we make it all the way to Orange Grove…

I like Miss Jane.

20
"THE SMOKING MOTHERS ARE CLAPPING"

It was Missus Wooster's idea…
To put on a puppet show in her backyard;
To set up a puppet stage,
Using a thick gray blanket,
And their redwood picnic table.
The Wooster Brothers,
Stevie, Robbie and Gary,
Will be the puppeteers. Who else?
And I get to be the puppet on strings,
The Mexican boy, who introduces the show.
Dennis Nelson and Kenny Stultz are now up the street,
Sent by Missus Wooster with promises of ice cream,
Spreading the word about the big show at noon.
I can see them going up the two sidewalks,
Kenny Stultz on the left, and Dennis Nelson on the right.

It is noon time and here they come.
There are at least a dozen little kids out there.
Their moms are standing back on the driveway,
Talking and smoking filtered cigarettes.
Now I see Missus Wooster talking with them.
She too lights a cigarette, and
Flicks her ashes into a beanbag ashtray.

Now they are all In line to pay their nickel.
Missus Sabatini is in line too wearing white shorts,

Helping little Scotty pay his nickel.
Walking up the driveway now is Missus Magehee,
Tugging at her daughter Nancy, to hurry along now,
To not be late to see the big puppet show,
Starring the Wooster Bothers: Stevie, Robbie and Gary.

I am good at this.
The little kids are actually laughing at my puppet.
Actually liking what I am doing back here,
As I dangle this wooden Mexican boy aloft,
Making this funny puppet dance in dumb circles,
Missus Wooster and Missus Sabatini clap their hands;
They are laughing out loud now,
As Stevie Wooster plays a phonograph record.
It's "Davy Crockett, King of the Wild Frontier."
The kids are singing along as Missus Sabatini sings too.

Now the Big Show has ended.
Dennis Nelson and Kenny Stultz are eating ice cream.
The children are happily cheering.
The smoking mothers are clapping.

INTERMISSION 2

CHRISTMAS ON MAVIS STREET, 1958.

THE AUTHOR IS FLEXING, AND FEELING BETTER AFTER THE FLU. ALSO PICTURED ARE THE AUTHOR'S GRANDMOTHER, UNCLE AND AUNT SEATED AT THE TABLE. THE MISTER IS FACING THE CAMERA, WEARING EYE-GLASSES.

21
"I CAN SEE ALL THIS WITHOUT MY CURTAIN"

The best time is now.
After school before the sun sets.
I am walking up the white sidewalk.
It feels good to look up this sidewalk,
Kind've like standing on a highway, and
Looking into the distance for miles.
I am walking with my Catholic shoes on,
Past the Sisson's.
I don't see Shirley and Rover today.
But I do see his red and black Studebaker.

Now I am coming to the Hilliard's house.
There is Missus Hilliard in her kitchen.
Her little kitchen window is always open.
She's getting dinner ready as usual.
I say Good Afternoon to her.

Now I am passing the Nelson's house.
Erik Nelson is on the front porch again,
Counting out the Mirror, secretly listening to KRLA.

Now as I look up this long white sidewalk,
I see the white stream ending.
Instead, I see the green ivy of Mister Gumm's yard.
There's Missus Carrell watering her grass again.
She is friendly and old.

Now she is walking to me.
She tells me to watch out for the nails,
Up ahead three houses;
The nails in Mister Gumm's yard,
Sticking up through a two-by-four, hidden, under his high ivy.
She says one of the Bliss girls stepped on a nail there;
Had to go to the hospital and get a shot.
She says the police were up there earlier.
I say thanks and decide to turn around.
The Missus already told me about this when I got home from school.
But I didn't believe it.
Now I do.

I'm not sure if I like Mister Gumm anymore.
I know he hates sidewalks.
And I know he doesn't like kids.
But, to hide nails in his ivy?
For kids to step on?
That is a mortal sin.

Here come the Nelsons now,
Driving down Mavis in their brown Rambler.
The Missus is driving with little Tina on her lap.
Now she is parking the station wagon.
Getting out from the backseats, I see
Sharon, Kathleen, and Valerie, all in
Catholic skirts with white socks; but not Tina.
She's in hand-me-down baby clothes,
As she runs inside the Nelson back door.

Now comes my friend and protector,
Riding his bike home from school;
Dennis Nelson says he's hungry for dinner.
He hopes it's not stew again.
He says he's been dreaming of fish sticks lately—
Says to come inside his house now.

Their house is a mess. There are laundry piles everywhere.
They look like haystacks from the rainbow;
Up to a dozen, maybe more.
There is no place to sit down in this house.
There are laundry piles on every chair,
On every sofa seat and table…

So I'm standing here, admiring
The Blessed Virgin statue by their front window.
I can see little roses in little vases there.
Now I can hear a radio coming from their hallway…
I am looking to see where the sound is coming from.
It's really close.
It's coming from the open bedroom on the left,
The one with a bloody dead Jesus on the wall;
Inside I can see the Missus prancing in slow motion,
Holding herself with eyes closed,
Dancing to the music of Mantovani.
My mom likes Mantovani too.
—the Anniversary Waltz…

I can see all this without my curtain.

22
"NOW THE MISSUS LIGHTS UP A SALEM"

I am leaving the Nelson house.
Dennis Nelson needs to do his homework.
He says he has thirty religion questions to answer.
I have twenty-two to answer, but I will forget to do it.
Answering religion questions is boring.

The sun is almost down now,
And all the Misters of Mavis Street,
Are driving their shiny Fords and Chevys,
And their brown Ramblers too,
Into the white driveways of their houses.
The day is done, except
Why are all the Stultzes sitting outside?
I see Wanda; Glenn, the twins, and Larry,
All sitting on their front yard,
As if waiting for the ice cream man.
Never seen that before.
I'm going up there to see what's going on…

Larry Stultz is walking towards me now.
He has a strange look on his face.
I ask why he and everyone else are all outside.
He says they are all locked out.
The Mister and the Missus did it.
He says they do this twice a month—
That they need to have their half-hour alone-time.

Usually they all wait in the backyard—
So no one knows.
But now all the neighbors know.
He says he's fine with everyone knowing.

I figure his parents are on their knees in there,
Praying hard to the Blessed Virgin Mary;
Praying hard for world peace,
Maybe praying for Kennedy too.
What else would they be doing?
Not sure if they're Catholic.
Maybe not.
I like the Stultzes.
But I am always hearing loud voices,
Coming out of their house.

It's dinner time at my house.
My mom has made Sloppy Joes.
I don't like Sloppy Joes.
But as the Missus would say—
"Tough luck, bad break."
I will eat it still.
As I sit here eating this stuff,
I ask my mom,
Why can't the Stultz kids pray with their parents?
My mom is confused.
I tell her they're all locked out;
They can't go in for thirty minutes,
Not while their parents are praying inside…
For world peace.

Now the Missus is looking out the dining room window,
The one facing the Stultz House.
My mother smiles and says praying is important.
That it must be done properly with a scapular.
Now the Missus lights up a Salem.

23
"THE MISTER PUTS DOWN HIS CROSSWORD PUZZLE"

It's dark outside now.
From the back porch,
I can see inside the Sisson windows.
Their bedroom lights are on,
So if I stand up on the porch railing,
I can see straight in.

Herbert's room is on the left.
He has a bunch of model airplanes,
Hanging by strings from the ceiling.
The middle window is Shirley's and Judy's bedroom.
I can tell because it's pink inside.
Their pink beds are fluffy-looking,
With a lot of clothes,
And stuffed animals on them.
Most of the time they have their shade down.
The window on the right is the parent's room.
Once in a while I see the Mister go in there.
He usually walks in to get something,
Then walks back out turning off the light.

Tonight my brother is shooting baskets.
He will do this for maybe a hour.
I like basketball.
Never played it before.
But I could learn.

My brother won't play with me though.
He thinks I ought to go bury myself,
And to leave him alone.
I think he likes Judy Sisson.
And I think he's shooting baskets out here,
To get her attention.
I would too if I was a old boy.
Judy has a big chest like Shirley.
That I know.

The Missus is in the kitchen right now.
She is wearing a beige dress with a apron on.
I like my mom in the kitchen.
That means she's baking something good to eat.
Her chocolate fudge is gooey and good.
That is what she is making now for dessert.

I ask her about Mister Gumm putting nails in his ivy.
Why would anyone do something as mean as that?
She shakes her head and says he needs to attend Mass.
Maybe if he received Holy Communion more often,
Then Mister Gumm wouldn't be such a terrible sinner.

The Mister is sitting in the front room now…
He's watching Wagon Train,
Still wearing his CPA tie.
I see him on the sofa now.
He's doing the TV Guide's crossword puzzle.
I can smell his feet because he has his shoes off.

Our black and white TV set
Is bright and flickering.
Sometimes the picture rolls
Like a slot machine.
That's when my mom usually says,"Heavens to Betsy,"
And I have to get up and adjust the vertical.
It happens a lot.

The Missus has wondered many times,
Whether the Koontz's are having problems too,
With their vertical as much as we are,
On their brand new RCA color TV set.
The Mister never answers her question.
He just quietly lights up another Pall Mall,
And continues to do his crossword puzzle…

I still remember the first time I watched a color TV.
It was on a Sunday night last summer.
Missus Koontz invited her girlfriends over,
And all their kids,
The Magehee's, the Woosters, the Hopes,
The Sabatinis, and my mom too—
Even Miss Jane was there…
To watch Walt Disney's Wonderful World of Color.

I never heard such oohing and aahing before.
There were women and kids all over the Koontz house,
Packed in there,
Like peanuts in a Payday bar,
Watching every cartoon character in action,

Without talking or even blinking it seemed;
No one wanted to miss anything.
Not even one second of all the color.

But that was nothing.
A week later on a hot afternoon,
Missus Koontz invited the same moms over—
This time, to catch the '62 All-Star game in color.
Luckily their kids were invited too.

The game was played in Washington DC.
Soon as Kennedy threw out the first ball,
I heard the oohing and the aahing.
I remember Missus Magehee and Missus Wooster.
They were the loudest ones to ooh and aah.

It wasn't long after that,
All the moms went into the kitchen,
Half dozen it seemed.
They started laughing like young girls.
Then they started lighting up cigarettes.
They smoked behind the kitchen door—
While we kids watched the game.
I like the smell of cigarette smoke.
I know then that they were good friends.
I was glad they were in there smoking.
I could see the TV better with them gone.

…Now my mom is bringing in the chocolate fudge.
The Mister puts down his crossword puzzle.

24
"IT FLIES AWAY WITHOUT ITS HEAD"

Today is a hot day.
This morning I can see Missus White.
She lives two houses down from us.
Most mornings she comes out to garden.
But she always comes out early.
She is a pretty lady.
I never see her talk to anyone,
Except for Eddie Magehee.
He lives across from her and they talk sometimes.
I try to talk to her too when I visit her flowers.
But she never comes out when I'm there.
She has blond hair and dark brown skin.
Her chest is like Missus Stultz's chest.
Not big, but not small.
I think Shirley Sisson's chest is much bigger.
That I know.

I like Missus White's flowers.
They're in the front yard by her windows.
Little butterflies fly around the blooms.
One day Eddie Magehee taught me how to catch them.
He said to wait,
Wait until they drink from the flower.
Then grab their wings.
Eddie Magehee also taught me how to tear their heads off,
And how to gently release them to fly away.

Which they do.

I think Missus White went inside…
I don't see her.
She's real pretty, but very shy.
There' s lots of butterflies here.
See. I got one. It's easy.
These things have two black eyes,
And a little black tongue that curls out.
There's stuff on my fingers from its wings.
Not sure what it is.
Here goes it's head.
Just like a tidily-wink.
And now, I let it go.
See.
It flies away without its head.

25
"FLEEING QUICKLY FROM THE IMPALA"

Time to go to school now.
It's 7:30.
Come on.
You can go with me today…
Look!
The Mister is backing up the Impala.
There is a lot of brown exhaust coming out.
My brother and Stevie Hope are riding in the backseat.
You can sit with them.

The Missus has given me my lunchbox—
"Voyage to the Bottom of the Sea"…
I know what's in there…
It's Wednesday and usually that means deviled ham.
But today is Hot Dog Day, so there are chips and a cupcake inside.
Everyone is in the Impala now.
I am in the front seat next to the Mister.
No. There are no seat belts.
The Mister is smoking a Pall Mall, as
I look inside my lunchbox for a cupcake.
Ah, there it is, a Hostess chocolate cupcake.
Now he turns on KRLA.
I like "Walk Right In."

As my dad drives down Mavis Street,
I wonder if I had homework last night.

I think this same thought everyday—
While passing the Magehee's house.
I recall that I had twenty-two religion questions to answer.

Here is Orange Grove Avenue.
The Mister looks both ways, then turns left.
There's Rockne Street.
A lot of mean kids live there.
I don't play on Rockne.

Now a right turn on Norwalk Boulevard.
Up ahead is the railroad overpass made of steel.
The Mister says kids go to jail for climbing up there.
Now we are turning left on El Rancho…

I hope school is not boring today.
But it always is.
Religion is the worst.
We answer questions from the Baltimore Catechism every day.
Sister in 4th grade said if we haven't memorized all the answers,
We are likely to end up in hell for eternity.
But answering questions is boring.
I have decided to take my chances and not memorize them.
That would be like hell itself.

Maybe Sister will take us to the church today.
Better to pray, than to study and work.
At least that's what I think.
It's not boring in the church.
Besides, God is testing us all the time.

Now we're passing Dennis the Menace Park.
I like the big slide and the swings.
There are picnic tables under shady trees everywhere.
I have seen over a hundred people at this park.
No one playing there now.

There's the Presbyterian Church on the left.
Stevie Hope and his family go there.
The plaque says "1949."
Next door is the new church under construction.
There are men working there now.
Stevie Hope says the church will open soon.
Maybe in June.

Now the Mister is making a left at Broadway.
The road curves here…
Across the street is Zestos.
I like Zestos—
Great snow cones and hot dogs there.

Now we are driving up Broadway.
There are big apartment buildings on this street.
One after another.
I see people inside the windows.
Their lights are glowing brightly.
I wonder who these people are.

I like the tall trees here…
They turn purple in the summer.
Now we are crossing the railroad tracks.

The Impala shakes for a second.
An ash from my dad's burning Pall Mall falls…
See?
It landed on the Mister's pants.

Now we make a right on Magnolia.
On the left is a junkyard for cars.
On the right is the miniature golf course.
I ask the Mister if we can golf there soon.
He says fine.

Now we turn left on Hadley.
KRLA is playing "Sukiyaki" on the radio,
As Stevie Hope tells the Mister he has a job—
Working on cars for Ack Miller…
In PR, over on the other side of the river.

Now we are turning down a side road.
On the left is the football field.
Now another left…
And up ahead are all the hot rod cars,
The cool cars, all parked by the gym.
My dad stops at the corner.
My brother and Stevie Hope step out,
Fleeing quickly from the Impala…

26
"I LIKE LIBRARY DAY"

The Mister turns east at Philadelphia Street.
Look to your left…
There's a good view now of the high school.
Those buildings look real old.
Even my parents went there a long time ago.
My mom says the buildings are as old as the hills.
But I like all the grass in front,
And I like the flagpole.

On the right now is an old mortuary.
Been there since 1919.
It's on their sign. See?
They have two black hearses parked in back.
I always see them when we drive by.
The building gives me the creeps.
I'm quite sure there are dead people inside it.

Now we are turning right on Pickering.
My school is coming up ahead.
There's the Safeway market on the left.
It's made of millions of bricks.
Same thing with Smith Hall, up there—
On old College Street.

Well, we're here.
The Mister is lighting his second Pall Mall,

As he turns the Impala left on College Street.
Look at all the Catholic kids,
Getting out of Chevies and Fords and Ramblers,
Running with book bags and lunch boxes.
They all look clean in their uniforms.
I just hope they all smell good.

Now the Mister is turning right on Newlin.
He stops at the curb.
He says to take the bus home today.
I like taking the bus home.
It's fun to stare out the window.

Time for school now in Room 12
It will be another normal day at St. Mary's.
First, we will all go to Mass.
I like going to Mass.
Everyday, except Saturdays,
I go to Mass.
When I go,
I wear my good Catholic shoes.
I wear my First Communion scapular.
I stare at the big cross behind the altar.
I watch Jesus hanging dead there.

When the girls choir sings,
I feel like I'm in heaven praying,
With all the saints and apostles,
As if they're all in the church singing too.
I like the organ music,

With Father Molthen up in the choir loft,
Waving his arm to the choir as he plays.

Today is a good day at school.
Not only is it Hot Dog Day,
It is Library Day too.
After Mass, we have Reading.
Then Math and Religion.
Lunchtime comes next.
Three Room Mothers will bring the hot dogs.
They also bring cupcakes and little milk cartons.
This is a good lunch time.
But like everyday for us,
We will all eat lunch inside the classroom, and
There will be silence.
We cannot talk.
When I eat at my desk,
I like to read Mine Magazine.
After twenty minutes of eating,
It is recess time outside on the parking lot.
We can all talk out there.

Today is real smoggy.
We probably won't go outside.
But then maybe we will go out.
When we do come back inside,
It will be Library Time.
All we do is read our books until 3 o'clock.
There is no studying or working.
Sister is not teaching.

We just take turns going to the library—
Five at a time for 15 minutes each.
It is free time.
I like to draw mazes on notebook paper.
Big Jeff Muller likes to solve them.
Most of the kids in class goof off, because
Sister Maria is at the library,
Making sure the five kids there are not goofing off.
I like Library Day.

27
"SHIRLEY SISSON HAS A BIGGER CHEST"

I am in my tree house now…
It is hot today.
The Missus has a small fan going in her kitchen.
I think she's making chicken and dumplings.
She has make-up on; more than usual.
Her lipstick is red.
Her dress today is beige-white.
She has on her black shoes.
The Missus is fat.
But she wears clothes that make her look skinny.
The Mister will like how she looks tonight.
He will also like my mom's chicken and dumplings.
That I know.

I like sitting up here.
Especially when it's hot outside.
You can feel the wind sailing through the leaves.
Like ghost spirits,
Kinda like playing soft drums with the oranges.
It's cool in the shade.
Think I'll go up to the top again.
When I'm up there, I can see in all directions.
I can see the neighbors in their backyards.
They are the most interesting.
Most of the time I see no one.
Just houses and trees, and the distant hills…

I am up here again.
I still have to be careful and hold on.
I can see City Hall in Los Angeles over there.
The Mister says it's sixteen miles away.
There's the Model, and the Beverly Fountain.
Now I see all those pine trees on Beverly.
They look just like an army of green giants.

Now I see the big play yard at Orange Grove.
There's the sandbox, and
The railroad tracks going across.
Wait.
I think I see…
There's someone over there…
Just a couple houses down from here…
I think it's Missus White in her backyard.
It sure looks like her.
She's suntanning…
Naked.
So it's true what everyone says…
My God.
She is all brown,
And she's got nothing on!
Wait 'till the guys hear about this…
I can hear her little transistor radio from up here.
It's KRLA…
Johnny Thunder is singing "Loop De Loop."
I am right.
Shirley Sisson has a bigger chest.

28
"HE SAYS KENNY STULTZ IS A LUCK-OUT"

The Tree Top Club is meeting soon.
I told the guys the reason for meeting was wicked,
And to come after dinner…
The Missus' chicken and dumplings tastes bland.
It has no flavor, but I do like the dumplings.
As the Missus says,
"It has good consistency."

The Mister is eating with his CPA tie still on.
The Missus is eating hers, wearing red lipstick.
I like the Missus' cooking.
But not her chicken and dumplings…

Now they both light up cigarettes and smoke.
I tell my mom smoking is bad.
She laughs and says she doesn't inhale the smoke.
I tell her I see Miss Jane smoking all the time on her front porch.
The Missus says Miss Jane doesn't inhale either.

Here they all come now on skidding bikes.
Dennis, Kenny, Randy, Larry, and
The Wooster Brothers, Stevie and Robbie—
All dashing into my backyard,
Here to find out the news of the sighting—
My sighting— of a nude Missus White in her backyard;
A real live sexy blond lady, like, Marilyn Monroe.

It felt good to know that I alone saw her naked.
That none of the guys saw what I saw…

But now the guys want to see her too.
If not now, then tomorrow, except,
Dennis Nelson says he can't get up there—
To the top of the tree;
Says he's too heavy, that the limb will snap.

Larry Stultz says he would go up for sures,
But why bother he asks,
If he's too small to see her once he's up there?
Same thing for Randy and the Woosters;
They can get up to the top like me,
But are too short to see anything—
Even on their tip-toes.
Only Kenny Stultz has the right height, the right weight,
To see this wondrous sight on tip-toe…
From the top of this old orange tree.

The sun is going down fast now.
The sky is fast losing it's brownish-orange curtain.
The guys are saying tomorrow after school—
Is a good time for Kenny Stultz to climb up there,
And then maybe see a nude Missus White,
Suntanning on her backyard recliner.

Larry Stultz is eating Milk Duds now.
After he swallows a mouthful,
He says Kenny Stultz is a luck-out.

29
"IT SEEMS THEY'RE SCRATCHING THE SKY"

The bus is half-filled with Catholic kids.
I like to sit about four seats back—
Always on the right side of the bus.
Sometimes the Nelson girls are on board.
Sometimes Missus Nelson picks them up in the Rambler.
I always see the Floro Brothers.
They live on Rockne.

We first go east on College Street.
I see old houses with old fences.
I see an old church on the corner of Comstock.
I see children outside playing in their yards.

Now we are turning left on Greenleaf,
Riding past the Hoover Hotel on the left…
The Bank of America Building on the right.
I see cars parked everywhere.
There are people walking in and out of JJ Newberry's.
I see old people and middle-aged people.
I see high school kids walking into the Owl Drug Store.

The bus in now heading north…
Passing Myers Department Store—
The high palms of Bailey and Hadley Streets, and
The picket fences on Broadway Street and Beverly Boulevard.
The bus driver is a skinny old man in gray uniform.

He is wearing glasses and a gray cap.
I like the bus driver, but he gets mad sometimes.
He tells the kids in back to sit down.
One time he stopped the bus on College Street.
He got up and went to the back to tell the kids there,
To "sit down and shut up."
They did.

Now we are turning west on Floro Avenue…
There are more old houses, more cross-streets—
With big shady trees, parked cars and telephone poles.
Now we are crossing Beverly again.
Behind me I can hear Sharon Nelson.
She is telling Kathleen Nelson: "It's Friday tomorrow—
There's no homework 'till Monday night."
Sharon is an eighth grader.
I think she likes my brother.
But then, maybe not.

Now we are passing Dexter Middle School.
Bobby Milan says he wants to go there.
He says the teachers at Dexter are nicer—
That they don't give homework in public schools.
I like Catholic school.
The kids are nicer at St. Mary's…

The skinny bus driver is turning right.
Now we are riding on Palm Avenue with all the palms trees.
Those things are really tall.
It seems they're scratching the sky.

30
"I'M HAPPY KENNY STULTZ IS STILL ALIVE"

Jeff Floro is sitting behind me today…
He is a funny kid.
I think he's in 3rd grade.
He talks a lot and
Calls me "freckled-faced foxy."
He says he lives by me on Rockne.
I don't like Rockne.
I have my reasons.

Now we're turning on Beverly again,
The third time…
Jeff Floro says he plays guitar and accordion—
That he and his brother Jerry have made a 45 record.
I don't believe him.

Riding down Norwalk Boulevard now,
Heading south to Orange Grove…
I see more cars and more houses,
More brick walls and more sidewalks.
Now the bus is swinging left to turn right.
The skinny bus driver is smiling, whistling…
As he makes a perfect turn.
Now he brings the bus to a stop at Rockne.
This is where the Nelsons and the Floros get off.
This is where I get off too…

Right now Jimmy Soul is singing on KRLA.
The radio in the kitchen is loud.
I like "If You Wanna Be Happy."
It makes me happy to hear it.

Today I am home from school.
I am faking it.
But as long as my mom thinks I'm sick,
Well, that's good too.
The TV dinner in the oven is bubbling.
The Mister went to the Model last night.
He bought milk, cokes, bread and my TV dinner.
It's a Swanson Loin of Pork…

The phone is ringing.
The Missus always picks it up.
She tells me it's Kenny Stultz.
This is the first time he's ever phoned me.
I answer it.
He says it's been a long time.
I ask him if his leg is better.
He answers that it was a bad break—
That it will take a lot of time before he can come out and play.
I tell Kenny Stultz again it's been ages.

Now he says to look out my dining room window.
I put the phone down and walk over.
I can see the Stultz house, but nothing else.
Why does he want me to look up there?
Oh, now I know why.

That's Kenny walking outside with a cane.
He's standing by the front porch light.
I haven't seen him since his fall from our treehouse.
I'm happy Kenny Stultz is still alive.

INTERMISSION 3

THE AUTHOR IS WITH HIS FRIEND, JIM THOMAS IN 1960.

IN THE BACKGROUND ARE THE HOUSES OF MAVIS STREET, AND MISTER SABATINI'S BLACK FORD PICK-UP TRUCK. FURTHER DOWN IS ORANGE GROVE. TO THE RIGHT IS MISSUS CARRELL'S PONTIAC, AND THE NELSON HOUSE.

31
"WHY ARE ALL YOU KIDS LOCKED OUT?"

These white sidewalks have heartbeats…
I can feel Life on these long little roads.
It seems Life is like a car.
Sometimes it goes forward;
Sometimes backward…
Right now I am going forward…

There seem to be loud voices up ahead.
I can see all the Stultzes inside their little garage.
I don't' see the Mister and the Missus.
Just the kids, locked out again.
Wanda Stultz looks upset and is yelling.

Now I see the crazy Jeffy Sabatini.
He's crying.
His mouth has blood coming out of it.
Larry Stultz is running up to me.
He says Jeffy climbed up on the Mister's workbench—
Says Jeffy fell and broke his front teeth.

Now I see Missus Sabatini,
Coming this way fast.
She does not look happy.
Little Scotty is right behind her.
Now Jeffy runs into her arms, crying still.
Wanda Stultz is talking to her.

Glenn Stultz is talking to her too.
But the rest of us are staying back.
Kathy is standing with her arms folded.
Kenny and Larry are cleaning up the blood…

There's Clint Tiernan riding his 10-Speed again.
Wanda Stultz sees him and stops talking.
She waves at Clint Tiernan who rides by with no hands.

Missus Sabatini talks a lot.
Now I can hear what she's saying.
"Where are your parents?"
—More talking and gesturing…

I wonder what my mom is making for dinner.
Maybe my dad will go to the Model Pantry for tacos.

Now Missus Sabatini is pointing at the Stultz garage.
She's wondering why it's open,
And why Mister Stultz is not around.
Now she's asking Wanda Stultz,
"Why are all you kids locked out?"

32
"I WANT EDDIE MAGEHEE'S BASEBALL CARDS"

I think I want to go home now.
Jeffy Sabatini is always getting into trouble.
One time I saw him playing on the roof of their house.
It's a miracle he's not in a wheelchair, or dead.

I'm hungry.
The sun is setting behind Orange Grove.
I see Missus Carrell watering her grass.
I wonder how old she is.
She must be in her seventies.
I say hello to her.
She tells me the ice cream man is coming—
That he is over on Adele right now.
I stop and listen…
Yes, she's right. I can hear him coming.

Eddie Magehee is walking towards me now.
He seems to be in a hurry.
He says to come over to his house.
All his baseball cards are for sale.
He has a lot of great star cards for a cheap price.
Now we're going into his backyard.
Inside his garage are two train sets.
I like train sets.
Wish I could play with mine.
I also see Mister Magehee.

He is bare-chested and lifting barbells.
I can hear Frank Ifield singing and yodeling—
From a black 45 record player—
"I Remember You."
Eddie Magehee says this song is the best song on KRLA.
He plays it again…
And again.

I am sitting in their back playroom.
There are outdoor chairs, pillows, and the record player.
Now Eddie Magehee brings out his shoe boxes—
Four full shoeboxes of baseball cards from 1958.
He says all his cards are on sale for 15 dollars.
I see a lot of Hank Aaron and Willie Mays cards.
His Yankee cards are good too…
He has three Mickey Mantle cards.
Now I hear Missus Magehee talking to the Mister.
She thinks the Mister has big muscles.
Now she's touching his arm as he flexes it.
Mister Magehee has bigger muscles than my dad.
But my father is smarter.

I tell Eddie I will ask my mother.
Eddie Magehee says he likes the Milwaukee Braves—
That he is sorry to let his Braves cards go.

Now I am crossing the street to go home.
My mom is in the front yard.
She says dinner is ready.
I ask what's for dinner.

She says two racks of spare ribs,
Marinading in Chris and Pitts barbecue sauce.
She is wearing her red dress today…
And earrings too.
Eddie Magehee tells her that I want to buy all his baseball cards—
For the "low price of 15 dollars."
She says "Sorry Eddie. Your price is too high."
I am truly sad.
I want Eddie Magehee's baseball cards.

33
"LIFE IS GOOD IN 1963"

The Missus is driving the Impala…
I am in the front seat looking out.
She's going to Hinshaw's,
The biggest department store at the Quad.
"Can't Get Used To Losing You" is on KRLA.
My mom thinks Andy Williams is a Catholic.
She taps her long red fingernails on the steering wheel…

As we drive down Painter Avenue,
Past the College and the Courthouse,
The Missus lights up a Salem cigarette.
She blows the smoke out the window.
She says the smog is getting worse outside.

Now we're coming to the Quad.
Once again she draws long on her Salem,
As she parks the Impala by the candy store.
And again, let's loose a cloud of white smoke.

With three large Hershey bars in her bag,
The Missus looks happy.
Hinshaws is a huge store inside.
It probably sells everything you could want.
It has a downstairs department too—
Filled with clothes, toys, games and music.
Now she sees a pink hat.

She stands in front of the tall mirror.
She tries on the hat and smiles.
I like her new hat.
It made her happy to buy it.
Now the Missus will cook a good dinner tonight.

My mom is parking the Impala at the Model.
She says the Mister wants T-Bone steak tonight.
So now she is going up the ramp carrying her purse.
I am outside in the Impala with the radio still on.
KRLA is blasting out the rock 'n roll sounds of 1963.
So far, I like 1963.

"Blame It On The Bossa Nova" is on now…
When I hear this,
I think of Patty Miller.
She sits in my row at St. Mary's.
Her blond hair is as white as the sidewalk.
Patty Miller is the tannest girl in Room 12—
—She's the perfect "surfer girl."
When I sit in class I stare at her.
And when I am not staring at her,
I imagine Patty Miller singing this wicked song.

…Now the Missus is coming down the ramp.
Ronnie Hope is carrying her bag.
As she gets in,
I ask, "What's for dinner?"
She says T-bone steaks and tater tots.
I like T-bone steak for dinner.

Now I ask what's for dessert.
She says hot fudge sundaes.
I like hot fudge sundaes a lot…

Perry Mason is on now.
The four of us are eating on TV trays—
Placed in front of our TV set.
My T-bone has a lot of Chris 'N Pitts sauce on it.
It looks like a pipe with blood covering it…

All the meat is gone now.
I am dipping the T-bone into the red sauce…
And smoking it like a real pipe.
The Mister is laughing at me.
He says I smoke a pipe better than his dad did.
The Missus tells the Mister to "hush now…"

The black and white TV is on in our dark house.
Sometimes I get a headache watching TV in the dark.
Della Street is looking at Perry Mason oddly.
She knows who killed the librarian…
An ad for Brylcreem is on now.
The Missus is reaching for a Salem.
The Mister, with lighter in hand,
Reaches over with a smile, and lights it.

It is past my 8:30 bedtime now…
The Defenders is on TV in the living room.
It is my mom's favorite program.
She says she likes Robert Reed's acting.

I can hear the Mister kidding the Missus now—
About chain-smoking during the show.
I can smell the smoke inside my bedroom.
Life is good in 1963.

34
"I ONCE WET MY PANTS IN 1956"

Dennis Nelson is here…
He's eating an orange as usual.
We're up in our treehouse today.
He says he's reading a spy book—
About a character named Bond.
He says it's wicked.
But he does not want his mom to find out…
Says he hides the paperback under his mattress.
Now he says he wants to start a new club.
A spy club…

The Mavis Street Spy Club.
That Is the name of our new club.
I thought of it.
We will spy on our neighbors—
Me, Dennis Nelson, Randy Koontz and Larry Stultz;
Maybe Kenny Stultz later on.

We will go out and hide at our neighbor's houses,
Hide behind trees and walls and chimneys.
We will look to see what we can see.
Dennis Nelson says we can never be seen.
Or heard.
He says he wants to spy on Missus White.
But not like Kenny did—
Being up at the top of that tree, then falling.

Now Larry Stultz says we should write stuff down.
I like that idea.

Dennis Nelson says we should go down to Orange Grove.
But not on bikes.
He says we can't be seen.

Our first stop is the Hilliard's house…
We are hiding in the bushes next door.
There's Kandace dancing in her white tutu.
She's playing a little record player on the front porch.
Larry Stultz says she's getting boobs on her.
Dennis Nelson says Larry shouldn't talk like that…

Now we are running down Mavis—
Passing by Miss Jane on her front porch—
Stopping now at the Magehee's.
We are on the side of their house…
Shhh… no one knows we're here…
Their bedroom window is open.
I can see the Mister with his bare chest;
He's wrestling with the Missus on their bed.
It sounds like he's smashing her because, well,
She's moaning a lot…
Hope she's okay.
Dennis Nelson looks in now.
He thinks we all need to go now.
He says this is not for kids to see.
I don't know what Dennis Nelson means.
With a yellow pencil in hand,

I write down what I just saw on a tablet…

Now we're running like crazy to Orange Grove…
I am the first to get there.
Kenny Stultz would have been first.
But he can't run.
Larry is last and is coughing a lot.

We are hiding behind the hedge now.
Though we can't see anyone yet,
We can hear voices…
Older voices, not kids' voices.
We are moving quickly to the voices.
They are coming from the drinking fountains—
Way over by the fifth-grade classrooms.
Dennis Nelson reminds us to be quiet…

Far as I can tell,
No one has seen us come here.
No one is even breathing loud.
But now,
Larry Stultz is dancing again.
He says he needs to pee bad.
I tell him, "Not here, not now."
Dennis Nelson is peeking around the corner.
He waves his hand to follow him…

"Look," he says.
We peek around the corner now.
And who do we see?

It's Shirley Sisson and Rover.
But they are not kissing.
They are standing by the fountain.
They are arguing loud like the Stultzes.
I can hear Rover telling Shirley to "shut up."
Holy cow!
Shirley Sisson has just slapped him.
I tell the guys "let's go now."
I don't like Rover.
If he catches us spying on them,
Well, I don't want that to happen.
Writing all this stuff down is not a good idea anymore.
As we leave, I notice Larry Stultz crying;
His blue shorts are wet with pee.
I tell him it's okay, that…
I once wet my pants in 1956.

35
"NOW I'M STANDING ON RANDY ROBERTSON'S FENCE"

It was Dennis Nelson's idea—
To disguise the Mavis Street Spy Club…
As butterfly catchers with nets.

Today the guys are at Randy Robertson's house.
There is a wooden fence there.
I like to stand on it and look out for butterflies.
It is also a good place to spy.

The Missus gave me two dollars to buy a net.
Me and the guys went to the El Mercado.
It's across the street from the Model.
We all got butterfly nets at the toy store.

Now I'm standing on Randy Robertson's fence…
I like the breeze blowing on my face when I stand here.
The Wooster Brothers are here,
So are Randy Koontz and Dennis Nelson.
Larry Stultz is standing on the fence behind me.
He is holding his green net with both hands.
I am looking upward to the tops of the big elms.
I am seeing the wind blowing through the branches.
He is asking if I've seen any monarchs.
I tell him no, not yet…

Here's Mister Robertson driving into the carport…

He always wears a suit to work.
Today he looks tired.
He has dark circles under his eyes.
He tells us to be careful as we stand on the fence.
We tell him we're on the lookout for monarchs.
He says they'll come because it's a sunny day…

Now I can hear music coming from inside their house.
Larry Stultz and I jump down.
We are walking quietly to the open screen door.
The music is louder now.
I've heard that song before on KRLA.
It's "Shut Down" by the Beach Boys.
Inside the screen door I can see Greg Robertson,
Randy's older brother, lifting barbells.
I think Greg Robertson is strong.
But not as strong or as big as Mister Magehee.
When the song plays again on his record player,
That's when he does his lifting…

Now the song's done.
Now he's done.
He's standing at the screen door.
Greg Robertson wants to know what we're doing.
I tell him I like "Shut Down."
"It's wicked."
But Greg Robertson says it's not wicked.
He says it's "cool."

Randy Robertson's big sister, Leigh,

Is in the front yard with her baton.
I think his sister is pretty.
But her chest is small.
She has black hair in a ponytail.
She is wearing her big white boots.
Over and over Greg Robertson plays that record.
We can hear it all the way out here.
Now Leigh Robertson is throwing her baton high,
And higher— so high,
I think it's gone higher than the house top,
And she still catches it.
I've decided that I like Leigh Robertson a lot.

Now I'm standing on Randy Robertson's fence…

36
"THIS IS THE CRUELEST THING I HAVE EVER SEEN"

Larry Stultz is yelling "Monarch, Monarch!"
He is pointing up to the top of that tree there,
The one in front of the Ghan's house.

There it is!
A big reddish orange one.
Now I am running down Mavis Street real fast.
I'm faster than all the guys in the club,
So this monarch is mine to catch…

Going past the Gumm, Stultz and Nelson houses…
He flies high and fast,
Like he's following the white sidewalks—
All the way down to Orange Grove,
Passing the Wooster, White and Magehee houses.
No cars coming so I cross the street.
I am running on the grass by the Kindergarten classroom.
My green net is open.
Now he's flying low by the bay window.
I aim my net…

It is night time now.
I am in my room listening to KRLA.
The Missus made meat loaf tonight.
She and the Mister talked about moving.
My mom wants to move in June.

But not to Baba's house.
Not unless she can paint the house first,
And get a new roof.
Of course the house will need to be fumigated.
The Mister said nothing.
Instead, he took out a Pall Mall cigarette and lit it.

KRLA is playing "Two Faces Have I."
I like this song.
But Lou Christie sounds like a woman.
The windows are wide open next door…
I can see the newlyweds sitting at their little table.
The young wife is facing her husband.
She is wearing a yellow dress.
I can see the metal zipper going down her back.

On my dresser is my pinning board.
I always kill and pin my catch.
I use half-inch black pins.
My pinning board is made of balsa wood.
It takes a day or two to ready the butterflies.
Then it goes into my glass display case.
My first monarch catch is now pinned there.
The guys were happy I caught it.
Dennis Nelson said I was a luck-out.

The Missus is in here now.
She is wearing an apron over her blue dress.
She wonders if I want to watch the Twilight Zone.
She says it's a good one tonight.

Now she is seeing my pinned monarch.
She thinks it is beautiful, but says,
"This poor thing isn't dead…"

I am staring at my monarch…
There are pins in its wings and body.
But my mom is right.
The monarch is trying to push the pin out of its body—
Struggling something awful,
With its long black legs—
It isn't dead.
The Missus is looking at me now…
She is pointing at my catch and says,
"Heavens to Mergatroyd…
This is the cruelest thing I have ever seen."

PART TWO

"TWILIGHT CONVOCATIONS" PAS DE DEUX

THE AUTHOR AND HIS BROTHER,
PICTURED WITH THE WHITE SIDEWALK OF MAVIS STREET IN THE BACKGROUND, 1959.

37
"I AM NOT ELEVEN YEARS OLD ANYMORE"

I am at Orange Grove by myself…
The guys can't come out to play yet.
It is morning still.
So, I am on the swing by the sandbox.
In the distance somewhere I can hear "Sleep Walk" playing.

This is a good place to sit and think.
For some weird reason,
I always think of my Willie Mays baseball card—
The one that came out in 1956.
It shows Willie sliding home safe.
That's how I want to always feel—
Safe at home.
But there are times when I think about death.
And what that's like.

From this swing I can see the whole school yard.
It's like an ocean of grass.
Sometimes I wish I can stay here for the rest of my life—
No school, no work and no bullies.
I turn to my right and I can see the railroad tracks.

I remember seeing my brother once,
Walking with Stevie Hope on those tracks,
Coming home from summer school classes—
My brother throwing a rock, then jumping the fence.

Erik Nelson used to play ball down here,
Over there, on those two baseball diamonds.
He could hit a baseball clear over the fence out there—
Even over the railroad tracks.

I remember the time a big dog chased Dennis Nelson.
He was scared something awful.
Just crying like a baby.
He was running everywhere down here—
His freckled face beet red and wet.
It was his brother Erik who chased that dog away.

Life is funny.
The stuff we don't want to remember,
We remember easily…

Now inside my mind I am feeling uneasy and strange…
It's as if I am being drugged by an invisible syringe.
The sky is bending and the sun is spinning—
How is this possible?
1963 is disappearing before my eyes…
Going away forever…
Like a fast-moving train to somewhere important…
Now I am having strange feelings inside my body…
It seems the movement of the earth is slowing down…
There is a grinding metallic sound in the sky…
I can feel the tug and the strain…
The years have disappeared into a vapor.
I am not eleven years old anymore…

38
"I AM SEEING GHOSTS ON THE WHITE SIDEWALKS"

I am walking…
I am 69 times around the yellow pancake.
It's 2021, and I live with my wife.
I was an English teacher for 38 years.
I have two daughters who are grown.
And I am back…
But why and how?

These old Mavis sidewalks are still white.
Listen!
Do you hear all those plodding footsteps?
There are plenty of ghosts here these days.
That I know.
But only on these blinding white sidewalks…

There's my old house.
Same driveway, same green lawn.
Ah, there's the window where my mom had her curtain.
Who is it, that's behind it now,
Looking out at the world and all its secrets?
He looks familiar.

There's my brother's old basketball hoop.
Still there on the garage roof.
Or maybe it isn't.
I swear I can hear his basketball dribbling.

But that can't be.
He has lived his life.
He's an old man of 74 years now.
He taught school for forty years.
How is it possible?
Look! He's talking to someone over the fence…
Is it Judy Sisson?

I am walking again…
My mind is vibrating like a motor.
Everything has changed, but
Everything has stayed the same.

The old elms are long gone.
They were perfect to sit under back in 1963;
The monarchs used to fly high above them.
Children's kites were eaten by them.
They've died out, and now,
Ash trees stand in their places…

There's the Sisson House.
It looks the same.
I wonder what happened to them.
I wonder if they are all dead now.

But wait.
There's Shirley and Rover,
Coming out of the house again.
They haven't changed at all.
Still young, and in love—

Still looking at each other like crazy teenagers.
Now I see Mister Sisson walking out of the house.
His black, ratted-up haircut hasn't changed one iota.
Is he looking for Shirley again, and
Her Studebaker-driving boyfriend?
Where are they?

I think I know…
They should be hiding by the side of their house—
Like they did every afternoon in 1963,
Finding privacy by the geraniums.
There they are…
Rover is smiling at her.
White angora still smothering his class ring—
The one on Shirley's right hand.
They are still exactly the same,
As if a single day has not passed by.
How is this possible?
Have I gone mad?

I keep walking up this white sidewalk…
I turn left, and once again,
I see Missus Hilliard.
She's looking out her little kitchen window,
Still making dinner at sunset,
Still keeping her eye on the neighborhood,
And on young Kandace…
Her little record player is still there—
Playing "Meditation From Thais" on the front porch…
Listen…

But Kandace is not here.
She's 71 years old now…
I wonder if she's still alive.

Now I see Missus Carrell with her husband.
This is something I can't explain.
I know they are both dead.
Been dead for decades, yet
She is watering the yard,
And he is touching up the house with a paint brush.
I want to say hello to them,
But I know they can't see me,
Nor can they hear my voice.
I am seeing ghosts on the white sidewalks.

39
"I CAN STILL HEAR THEM SCREAMING AT EACH OTHER"

Shh…Listen…
The music in the distance…
I have heard it before.
"Our Winter Love" by Bill Pursell…
It's coming from the old Stultz House.
They moved out of that house in 1963,
Right after we moved out of ours in June.
So, I wonder if maybe…

Good God almighty…
I see Kenny Stultz sitting on the front porch.
Just like he did 58 years ago;
He's still 12 years old, with that cast on his leg.
The front door is ajar…
The music is coming from a record player inside.
He can't see me as I pass by…
He's just sitting there, oblivious…
Looking across the street at something.
He must be a ghost.
Is Kenny Stultz dead now?
I can smell ground round patties sizzling on a stove…

There's Missus Stultz lying on her sofa—
32 years old again with five children,
Living in a tiny house with one bathroom.
She is in her faded swimsuit and wearing eye-glasses.

She's reading Reader's Digest with her skinny legs spread open—
Her black pubic hair is sticking out like worms.
Now the Mister storms in like his B-17.
He orders the Missus to clean up the mess.
He says the house is a damn pigsty.
Their loud cussing hurts my ears…

But she and the Mister are decades dead.
This argument isn't really happening…
Or is it?
Yet somehow, as I walk away,
I can still hear them screaming at each other.

40
"DENNIS NELSON IS DRESSED IN HIS FUNERAL SUIT"

…Now I see the Nelsons driving down Mavis…
Driving that old Rambler station wagon again.
Where's the family?
Missus Nelson is gripping the steering wheel—
Bringing the Rambler into their driveway,
Her bright auburn hair gleaming still;
But… she died many years ago.
Sometime in the 90's…
In the backseat I see Dennis Nelson eating an orange.
Why is he alone back there?
Where are the girls?

Is it even possible that,
He and the Missus now are but neighborhood ghosts here?
But only to my eyes,
Visiting me here now, from the distant past?
Why is this happening?

Dennis Nelson is wearing that same suit;
The one he wore in his casket…
All the Nelsons were inside St. Mary's Church…
That hot August day in 1970—
The day they buried Dennis Nelson at age 19.
I heard it was leukemia.
He was my friend and protector.
I was there for him in 1970—

Because Dennis Nelson was there for me…

…Close your eyes now…go back…
Summer of '62; we were playing bike tag—
Dennis Nelson and me—
At Orange Grove's Ocean of Grass.
We'd been riding fast that afternoon,
Whisking down all the walkways like jets—
All the cool corridors and the asphalt pavements,
When suddenly,
Allan Raggio and Brent Traft struck like thieves…

They lived over on the mean streets—
Rockne Avenue and Carley;
They were the bullies of the block.
No other kids around these parts,
Had as much mischief on their minds,
As these two sixth graders did in 1962;
They terrorized Orange Grove on their Sting-rays.

As I got off my Schwinn to get the beanbag,
Allan Raggio appeared like a roving monster.
Silver-haired and tanned, he yelled, "Get him!"
Then from behind, the sneaky Brent Traft
Accosted me with a strong bear hug.
As he held me,
Allan Raggio started lighting matches.
Then he started throwing them at me.
The two boys laughed while I screamed.
Then with monstrous intent,

Allan Raggio tried to light my tires on fire.
Terrified, I ran away from them,
Leaving my bike with the bully, Alan Raggio.

My friend and protector,
Dennis Nelson, then rode up on his bike.
He skidded on the cement with a high screech.
He then told Alan to back off,
And to leave my bike alone, or he would tell.
Alan Raggio spat on the ground and laughed.
He knew Dennis Nelson wasn't afraid of him.
"Go on and tell your mamas," he said. "I don't care."
He and the sneaky Brent Traft then backed off,
Laughing like little kids,
As they rode away on their mean sting-rays…

I was relieved I got my bike back.
And I was happy I was not burned.
Dennis Nelson stood by me that day.
As we walked our bikes up the sidewalk,
I recall I was still sniffing.
So Dennis Nelson explained everything that happened to my mom.
The Missus thanked Dennis Nelson after hearing the story.
As we walked away from the kitchen,
She promised to have a "little talk with their moms soon."
She did.

…Now I see him in 2021,
Walking on Mavis Street again…
Dennis Nelson is dressed In his funeral suit

INTERMISSION 4

THE MAVIS STREET SPY CLUB IN ACTION.
DENNIS NELSON, ARMED AND ON PATROL - 1963

41
"LIFE WAS GOOD IN 1957"

…The black Ford pickup is gone now.
Mister Sabatini drove it to work everyday in 1963.
He always parked it right here—
In front of their house by a big Elm tree.
He used to drive up Mavis with little Scotty on his lap.
Jeffy used to sit inside it, turning the steering wheel—
Even on hot summer days.
But now,
On the old asphalt, lay the oiled remains;
Still oozing after fifty-eight summers…

To my left I see that same kitchen window—
Now it is closed and dark.
But inside my remembering mind,
I can again see the way it was.
Close your eyes now…

I wonder if she's there…
Missus Sabatini, inside her kitchen.
I look and I think I can see her…
I want to see her,
Just as she was, with that mysterious smile.
I think I can hear her.
Shhh….
She's telling Jeffy and Scotty to sit down;
Forever telling the boys to mind her…

There she is—
I can see her; she's still young and spry—
She's playing the radio in her kitchen—
KRLA in the afternoon…
She still has that look on her face—
Still gazing out that same window.
Little Peggy March is singing "Johnny Cool"—
Missus Sabatini is singing along as she cooks dinner.

Open your eyes now…
Am walking on this sidewalk again.
I need to keep moving, keep watching.
The Hopes are not home.
They haven't been for 45 years.
The old blue paint still perspires,
Still glistens, as the house abides—
Facing the insistent west.
The old garage that was always open in 1963,
Is now closed and locked.
The white sidewalk out front,
Discloses another hour in its waking time…
Close your eyes…

Mister Hope is in his garage working,
His tall sons stand at his side,
Handing him clean tools and dirty rags…
The radio is blaring on a clear morning in 1957…
"Teddy Bear" by Elvis is coming out of the speakers.
Missus Hope is cooking breakfast in her tiny kitchen.
I smell bacon frying as she waves through the kitchen window.

I wave back thinking she can see me.
She can't.
Her four children are now seated at the kitchen table,
Staring like mannequins with no movement,
Eternally waiting for pancakes and bacon.
Johnny Ace comes on the radio now…

I had forgotten.
Life was good in 1957…

42
"THESE TWILIGHT CONVOCATIONS HAVEN'T ENDED"

…Dennis Nelson and me are up in the tree house…
He has on his Cub Scout tee-shirt and blue jeans.
He's eating a big orange.
The summer of '62 has gone by fast.
But now in August, our mood has changed.
We heard today about Marilyn Monroe…

Dennis Nelson thinks she was murdered by the Mafia.
I think what my mother thinks:
She swallowed too many sleeping pills.
Dennis Nelson says you never know when death will happen.
He says death drops in when you least expect it,
Like a distant cousin coming to call unannounced.
I tell him I pray to Jesus, Mary and Joseph everyday.
He says you can pray all night, but if it's time, it's time…

I look up to the highest branch now.
I can see the blue sky behind the leaves.
Now I feel a shifting of the elements,
As if the massive turning of the earth has stopped.
Overhead I hear a silver Constellation flying by…

I stare at Dennis Nelson's ghost now—
Sitting there as a grinning spirit,
12 years old with freckles, and fat still.
I feel a warm wind blowing through the orange blossoms.

I close my eyes tightly…

…Now I find myself inside St. Mary's church,
The green suede doors are opening up for me like magic,
Like a miracle leaping out of my old catechism—
I walk forward as I did on First Communion day in 1960…
Mmmm…I can smell the burning frankincense in the air.
The church is filled with dressed-up Catholics today.
The Mister and the Missus are in the back, waving.
My mother is wearing her blue dress and a white hat.

Now I open my eyes… But I'm still here…
The wooden pews today are cold and empty.
The stained glass windows are letting in just a little sunlight.
Up ahead there, I can see an open casket…
Now the Girls Choir is singing softly in Latin.
All-around me I see the Stations of the Cross—
The flickering funeral candles casting gray shadows.
I turn my eyes to the center aisle…
Now Dennis Nelson is sitting up in his casket wearing his funeral suit…
The Girls Choir is singing low in a long sustained tone…
Dennis Nelson says he wants Twinkies…

These twilight convocations haven't ended.

43
"I LEARNED MANY THINGS FROM MY MOTHER"

…Kenny Stultz is here now.
Hasn't changed a bit since 1963.
He still likes to sit up on the highest branch.
I sit second highest, then Dennis Nelson.
Larry Stultz sits at the bottom.
But today the guys aren't here.
Just Kenny Stultz.

I am happy to see him again.
Even if he is just a haunting from 58 years ago.
I choose to go along with these curious apparitions—
This rush back to when life flowed differently.
Today Kenny Stultz is going to the top.
Just as he did back in 1963,
When he climbed up to my branch in the sky…

… He made it up there this time;
Kenny Stultz can now see what I saw;
Feel what I felt when I was up there so long ago.
I'm happy he can see Missus White now—
Forever suntanning in the nude.
Though decades dead in the graveyard…
He says he "can see her, that
She's reading something, and wearing nothing."
Now he says "bitchen."
I'm happy my tree branch held him this time—

That he didn't fall fifteen feet to the ground.
"I can hear her little radio," Kenny Stultz says.
"She's listening to 'Johnny Get Angry'"…

…It is dinner time.
My mother died in 2003, but now,
She's in the kitchen, as she was,
Standing by the stove listening to KRLA…
"Cast Your Fate To The Wind" is playing.
My God, she is so young-looking—
And she is not fat at all.
I thought she was back then—
Because the guys said she was.
But now, seeing her in 2021,
I change my mind.
Her face is pretty, and so alive.
She has on eye make-up and red lipstick.
She's wearing her blue dress but I can't see her shoes.
There is a strange gauze-like cloud covering them.
A white apron made in Mexico is around her waist.
I can smell meat loaf in the oven.
Soon my dad will be coming home from work.
Soon the TV will be on,
Showing the Huntley-Brinkley Report on Channel 4.

My mother is beautiful, and very high class,
Even as she rules over this middle-class household.
How does she do it everyday?

Now she's stepping outside on the back porch,

Lighting up a Salem, telling me dinner's ready—
To "come in right now."
Then adding, "And I don't mean maybe…"

I go into my room to change my shirt.
Through my second window I can see the newlyweds next door—
Forever sitting at their little kitchen table…
Eating in silence…

Again my mother tells me to come and dish up now.
I had forgotten about her absolute rule over me.
But to be honest,
I learned many things from my mother.

44
"I ASKED IF I WAS STILL DREAMING"

…There was that awful time,
In 1958… I caught the flu during Christmas.
My fever was over one hundred two.
The vomit that came out was brownish red.
Three times it rushed out of me like hot soup.
One time I barfed on the Mister.

But on that December night so long ago,
The Missus sat in her big red chair for hours,
Holding and rocking her very sick boy…
I can still hear the music she was playing.
Listen… The Mitch Miller Gang is singing in stereophonic sound,
"We Three Kings…"

Then it was Christmas morning finally…
The house on Mavis Street was awake—
Lit up with flickering candles,
The green tree in front of the window—
Aglow with lights and silver tinsel;
I walked into this magical living room and I saw it—
The little HO train set running fast and smooth,
Over small black electrical tracks,
Through a little plastic town set up by my dad.
I remember thinking it was magnificent.
I asked if it was mine.
I asked if I was still dreaming…

45
"BACK TO WHEN LIFE TURNED DIFFERENTLY"

…Jimmy Dorsey is playing "Sophisticated Swing."
I can hear him down the street—
His sax sound is coming out of someone's house,
Like a siren's call to walk down there and visit.
But all my neighbors from 1963 moved out decades ago.
Most of them are decades dead…

Now I see the door open at the Magehee's house…
Close your eyes…
I see Missus Magehee alive again in her thirties.
It is 1963…
She's sitting on her sofa smoking a Newport cigarette—
Her red hair beaming like Chris and Pitts steak sauce.
She's looking out the window,
Waiting for her husband to come home from work…
Puffing nervously now.

Jimmy Dorsey has the afternoon mood under his control.
He's playing "So Rare" now.
He knows the Mister will be pleased at how clean,
How tidy, the Missus has kept the house today.
There may be rewards given—
Before the children come in.
There may come curious sounds from their bedroom window,
Like a ribbon turning loudly inside a typewriter…

Now she reaches into her purse for lipstick.
Mister Magehee has just parked the Buick in the driveway.
Missus Magehee knows the time has come—
To dim the lights…

Decades dead she is—
The music though, still soars through these tall trees—
And In between these small houses,
Mixing in with the voices of ghost children—
Ever reminding me of a dead woman's desire,
Back in the distant good times,
Back to when life turned differently…

46
"HEY MISTER GUMM. ANY EXTRAS?"

What is Missus Carrell doing?
Instead of watering her grass,
She's hosing the gutter in the street.
That's odd.

I walk up to her thinking she's still alive,
But Missus Carrell does not see me.
Nor is she aware of what she's doing.
She's like all the rest of them.
Missus Carrell is a dead person forever alive—
Forever haunting this old street.

Why is she watering there?
I am looking closer now and can't believe my eyes.
Flowing down Mavis Street I see a stream of blood,
Surging strangely from Mister Gumm's house.
I squint my eyes now and search for its human source.
Wait…
I can see someone.
Is that Mister Gumm up there—
Sitting with his feet hanging over the curbside?

I am now quickly walking up the white sidewalk…
I am wondering if Mister Gumm is dying.
But how can that be if he's been dead for decades?
Now I see him sitting in his overgrown ivy;

His puffy hands covering his pained face.
I believe the man is crying…
I can hear his sobs as he sits there.

Now I can see why he is bleeding.
Good God, this is a sickening sight…
Both of his bare feet have long nails sticking through them—
His nails—
The same ones he used to hurt the Bliss girl.
Now he is gushing blood non-stop,
Bleeding forever in the gutter.
I look at him there and I tell him I don't like him.
I tell him, 'what goes around comes around.'
But he can't hear me either.
He's just a dead man no one wants to remember.
I am walking away from him now.
But I have one more thing to say to him:
"Hey Mister Gumm. Any extras?"

47
"I SEE A PALL MALL CIGARETTE DANGLING FROM HIS LIPS"

…These white sidewalks speak silently.
I can hear a thousand scooter wheels,
Darting fast over crack and easement—
Heading down to Orange Grove and the railroad tracks,
Carrying the conversations of vanished ten year-olds;
The Ocean of Grass lies beyond like heaven,
Like a promised paradise my father earned fighting the war…

I can see the tall elms that once stood here—
They were indeed quiet friends,
Especially in the summer times of Catholic innocence,
Of cool refuge in the games of determined pursuit…
I continue to be amazed at what I see…

Is that Eddie Magehee standing in front of Missus White's house?
Good God, he's an old man now—
He's still catching the butterflies in her old garden there…
Still ripping their tiny, black-eyed heads off…
One after the other without stopping,
And letting them fly away to a dark death.
There is no life in Eddie Magehee now—
He is just a body that looks dead, but is still moving.
Like a stone statue with a fake heartbeat.

I am wondering now what will happen to me after I die.
Will I be punished by God for my sins—

Doing something horrible like this...
For eternity?
I pray to Jesus, Mary and Joseph that does not happen...

Now I see someone coming my way from Beverly.
Coming on a 10-Speed bike, riding it with no hands—
It's Clint Tiernan riding smoothly down Mavis again,
And forever...
Looking to get a glimpse of Wanda Stultz,
Standing in her sundress by the front yard tree,
Her long blond hair waving in the wind...

There's Missus Koontz talking to Missus Wooster...
How odd this is...
They are floating on a cloud over the white sidewalk.
It seems these ghosts are part somewhere, part nowhere...
Both are wearing tight shorts and swimsuit tops;
Both are smoking cigarettes, unaware they are floating,
Unaware they are decades dead...

Missus Wooster is telling Missus Koontz she'll be moving soon.
They have bought a house in Newport Beach.
They will have a cabin cruiser parked in their own dock.
Missus Koontz lights up another cigarette.
She says she's happy for Missus Wooster and the boys;
She says life at the beach will be like "heaven on earth."
I see them embracing and kissing fifty-eight years ago...
Mister Wooster is home now in the family station wagon.
Missus Koontz walks away to her green disappearing house...

Now the sun is setting behind Orange Grove.
I can hear a silver Constellation flying overhead.
I can smell hamburgers frying in these small kitchens here.
Popeye is broadcasting on these black and white televisions,
All plugged into the plaster walls of these small houses.
Look, there's my dad.
He's driving up Mavis Street in his blue '58 Impala…
I see a Pall Mall cigarette dangling from his lips.

48
"LIFE IS WICKED, MAN. REMEMBER THAT"

This is the best of part of my life—
When my dad comes home from work;
The very minute his Impala enters our driveway.
The loose tie and white shirt…
The black ledgers…
The six pack of Coke…
The baseball cards in his shirt pocket…
This is when I know life is good and safe…

My mother is attired in her blue dress, with red lipstick.
She's playing KRLA loud today.
"Rhythm of the Rain" is on…
Now's she's kissing the Mister with practiced affection.
She tells him they're having chocolate fudge for dessert tonight.
He grabs the Missus by the arm.
He takes her into the bedroom.

I hear nothing but KRLA for about fifteen minutes…
Now they are coming out.
He has his hand on the small of her back…

Indeed, this is the best moment—
The best time in anyone's life.
My parents are young again, and in love.
Best of all,
There is a meat loaf from heaven being served tonight…

But now I realize this scene, this vision,
Is just a clear blur,
Quilted together to show how it was,
Like an old movie,
When being alive turned differently in 1963…
When I knew everything would be okay in life;
—That I was ready to explore the curious places,
The compelling mysterious places,
All very much out in the open on Mavis Street.

Who is that walking this way?
Walking through the vapor, which hovers
Like a cloud above the white sidewalks?
I see Larry Stultz, coming to meet me,
To listen to me,
As I tell him how fleeting life is;
To let him know,
These times are the best times…

Larry Stultz is ten years old again.
But all he does now is just stare at me—
He says nothing.
Now I hear ghost music coming from the Stultz house,
Dave Baby Cortez is playing the "Happy Organ"—
I can imagine Larry's mom in that house now…
Lounging for eternity in her faded pink swimsuit…

"…Larry, you're just a kid.
But right now, in May of 1963,
This is the best time of your life.

Believe me!
It gets bad, and after it gets bad,
It all goes down hill…
The Vietnam War, the riots and the assassinations—
The flag-draped body bags.
These will all come your way.
Larry, you're just a kid and you don't know yet…

Look at that sunset.
Man, that is wicked, isn't it?
Sometimes I think I can see God in the sunset.
Can't you?
Then other times I think of dinner, and
What mom's making on her gas range tonight.
Just walking into her kitchen is a good thing.
Just like this sunset—
Something to behold.
Larry, I just wanted to tell you it's all good,
No matter how bad it gets,
Life is wicked, man. Remember that."

49
"I FINALLY TELL JEFF SABATINI I'M SORRY"

…I'm walking on this sidewalk again…
In the distance —
I hear "Sleep Walk" playing on someone's record player.
The old elm trees are back on Mavis Street,
As they were.
I can see the mourning cloaks sleeping…
Forever sleeping—
On the gray outstretched branches.

As I near the Hope's house,
I notice a movement in the corner of my eye…
There's someone…
Someone's sitting inside Mister Sabatini's black truck.
Who is that behind the steering wheel—
Pretending to drive it like a grown-up?
I walk up to the side window now.
I see Jeffy Sabatini gripping the wheel.
He is oblivious, and staring straight ahead…
His dark olive complexion gleams like sea mist.

I want to tell him I'm sorry—
Tell him it was wrong—
To make him play the dead Jap all the time;
That it was mean of me and the guys—
To ditch him at Orange Grove all the time.
I can't explain why we picked on him.

We just did.
And now, as he sits frozen forever…
Inside his father's old Ford truck,
I finally tell Jeff Sabatini "I'm sorry."

50
"IN THE MIDDLE OF THE OLD MODEL MARKET PARKING LOT"

It's 1963 now…
I'm riding in the Impala with the Missus…
She needs to go to the Model for bread, deviled ham and cokes.
I cannot believe I'm doing this again.
I love every second of it.
She lights up a Salem after she parks the car.
I had forgotten how often my mother smoked back then…

…There's Hope Robertson coming out of the Model now.
Box-boy eternal, Ronnie Hope, walks behind her.
He's carrying two grocery bags in his arms.
I see a loaf of Wonder Bread inside one of them—
A box of Hostess Twinkies in the other.
But this can't be…
The Model was torn down thirty-five years ago.
All the people who worked there are dead now…

Now I see a vision that is utterly remarkable;
It's Patty Miller in a white bikini.
Coming down the ramp in high heels…
Holding a silver microphone—
Her booming voice coming through the Model loudspeakers;
She is singing "Blame It On The Bossa Nova" as she dances.
All the moms in the parking lot get out of their cars and dance too…
When the song is over,
The Mavis moms light up filter-tipped cigarettes…

Again, I understand these spiritual interludes—
These somewhat crazy illuminations of Mavis Street in 1963…
But I wish to close my eyes now. Please.
They grow tired and heavy.
I need to rest my mind from these urgent and remarkable visions.
Maybe Mister Serling can come out of the shadows now—
Smoking his smoldering cigarette.
But I cannot resist.
These visions flow before me like a strong river…

…Now from the backseat of the '58 Impala,
I can see Hope Robertson crying inside her station wagon—
Two parking spaces over by the ramp.
The Missus says Mister Robertson died yesterday.
He had a heart attack at work.

Now the Missus is getting out of the Impala.
She says she's going to Hope Robertson to console her.
I can hear Ray Charles singing "You Don't Know Me" on KRLA,
As my mom and Hope Robertson hug for eternity—
In the middle of the old Model Market parking lot.

51
"THEY WILL TELL YOU VOLUMES IN SILENCE"

…Now, this is not true,
It didn't happen this way—
The time Randy Robertson gave me a Duke Snider card.
But here he comes…
From the backseat of their station wagon.
Now he's walking to the Impala—
Walking past our hugging mothers.
He's holding the 1956 baseball card of Snider.
Do my eyes really see this?

Now he's knocking on my window.
Slowly I turn the handle to roll it down.
"Here's the Snider you wanted," he says.
I say thanks, and roll up the window.
But I tell you, it did not go that way, no.

Instead, I was standing on the Robertson fence—
My eyes on the lookout for a monarch butterfly.
Greg Robertson was lifting barbells inside their front door—
His loud record player playing "Shut Down."
He told me to always say "cool" when life goes good.
"Don't say wicked, man," he said,
"That's not cool anymore."

Then as I was leaving with Larry Stultz,
Here comes Randy Robertson with the Snider card.

"I hear you need this card," he says.
"You can have it."
"Thanks, man."

But does it really matter how it all happened?
No.
It was and is inconsequential.
The Snider card was just a gift from a kid—
To a kid,
A long time ago in 1963…
On a shady suburban street in Los Angeles County,
When life turned differently…

There I am.
Sitting on the curb with Larry Stultz,
Staring at my new Snider card.
Behind us is Leigh Robertson in majorette boots,
Throwing her baton a mile up into the sky…

I have thought back often in my life,
Recalling that moment—
Of rare generosity between children.
There are souls who might remember…
Children, now grown old,
Who still haunt these old Mavis sidewalks.
Ask them if life was cool back then.
They will tell you volumes in silence.

52
"THE VAPOR IS GONE"

I am walking…
But I cannot see my feet.
I am walking on this old sidewalk yet again…but
There is that same odd-looking vapor concealing the cement.
I can feel the ground, but I cannot see it.

I turn my head now and
Up the street a ways,
I can see someone floating on a gauzy cloud…
Hovering above the ground like magic.
Amazing.
It's an old woman dressed in green,
Coming this way…

Who is it?
Now I hear the singing voice of Johnny Ray,
Soaring like a lost ghost up in the Elms…
"Walking My Baby Back Home"…

Good God Almighty…
It's Miss Jane.
She's awful looking—
Not the way she was in 1963…
Back then she was young and pretty…

Now the vapor is bringing Miss Jane down to the ground—

I can see her skinny legs and emaciated body.
Her face is very old and pale.
Miss Jane is dying of cancer.
I am sad to see her like this…

Now she gestures for me to take her thin arm…
I do, putting it through mine;
And this is as it should be…
We are walking together back home…

Her Sky-Birds now are drenching us with cool water.
Miss Jane is sopping wet as we stand there.
I look away because she wears the awful face of death…

Now Johnny Ray is singing in the trees again—
The turning of the earth subsides for a minute…
I can feel the tug and the strain like before.
There is that same metallic grinding sound in the sky.
Miss Jane is being devoured by a bright eating light…
I see tiny exploding filaments all over her body—
I cannot believe my eyes…

Miss Jane is now as she should be— eternally young in 1963.
The vapor is gone.

53
"I LIKE MY DAD"

Shh…listen…
Someone is playing their record player—
"Sleep Walk" by Santo and Johnny.
That is beautiful music, isn't it?
Come and sit under this shady elm.
We can rest here and listen to the music.
We can remember life as it was in simpler times—
When silver Constellations streaked these skies.
I recall their loud roarings in the blue distance.

Now I can see my brother and Stevie Hope—
Riding their bikes up the white sidewalk,
Riding like cowboys on the lonesome trail,
Riding forever inside my old mind,
In and out of the reaching elm shadows,
Moving fast to Beverly, and the El Mercado…

All around us I see sleeping cars parked;
Fords, Chevies, Pontiacs and Buicks;
All reaping in the yellow smog and the sun,
All hiding slick oil stains on the graying asphalt…

Life is just a stroll on a white sidewalk—
Every scene and sound a private mirror in time.
I have purchased it all with cupcakes and memorized prayers.
Time now to drink this soul elixir from this ancient cup.

I dared the ghosts here to come out and show themselves.
I dared them to show me their regretful shadows.
I close my eyes again…

So this is what happens after my last breath…
I'm just a walking dead kid,
Come to haunt the living like all the rest here—
Forever 11 years old in 1963, on old Mavis Street;
This is the heaven of my soul's being…

…Now I see the Mister rounding the corner at Beverly—
Tiptoeing one foot at a time on the curb…
Coming down Mavis Street on a gauzy cloud.

My dad died in 2005.
He was eighty-eight times around the yellow pancake.

…He sees me now on the grass; he's waving.
My dad is forever home.
He has a pack of 1956 baseball cards in his shirt pocket.
I like my dad.

CODA

MAVIS STREET 1960.
PICTURED IN THIS SHOT: THE AUTHOR, DENNIS NELSON, IN CUB SCOUT TEESHIRT; PATTY MILLER (FROM ADELE STREET); ERIK NELSON AND THE AUTHOR'S BROTHER, PAUL.

STARK HUNTER

PICTURED IS THE AUTHOR (ASLEEP)
WITH HIS GRANDDAUGHTER, EVALYN. 2020.

ABOUT THE AUTHOR

BORN IN WHITTIER, CALIFORNIA IN 1952, Stark Hunter was an English teacher for 38 years before retiring from the classroom in 2017. He has written and published 10 books, which are available on Amazon.com and Barnes & Noble.com: In A Gadda Da Vida, a novel, published in 2002, Carnivorous Avenues, a poetry volume published in 2004, Flies, a short novel published in 2005, Private Diaries, a satire published in 2006, Voices From Clark Cemetery, a poetry volume published in 2013, Cocktails For the Soul, a poetry anthology published in 2013, Voices From Mt. Olive Cemetery, a poetry volume published in 2018, Digested by the Dust, another poetry anthology, published in 2018, Scenes From the Cerebellum, published in 2019, and Monster Trees, published in 2020.

Mr. Hunter's poetry has been included in the following Poetry Anthologies: Stars In Our Hearts, Visions, published 2012 (World Poetry Movement); In My Lifetime, Chronicles, published 2013 (Eber and Wein Publishing); PS: It's Poetry, An Anthology Of Eclectic Contemporary Poems Written By Poets From Around the Globe, published 2020 (PoetrySoup.Com).

Fourteen of Mr. Hunter's poems from Voices From Clark Cemetery were adopted and set to music by Dr. George Mabry, composer and former conductor of the Nashville Symphony Chorus, for his work, Voices, a musical drama which was performed at Austin Peay State University in Clarksville, Tennessee in 2015.

Three of the author's poems were read on Diverse TV with host, Alexandro Botelho, for his program, "Live Writings On The Wall" in 2021.

www.ingramcontent.com/pod-product-compliance
Lightning Source LLC
Chambersburg PA
CBHW020935090426
42736CB00010B/1144